"WATCH MY PROPHESIES."

© *2016, 2020*
CALIFA MEDIA PUBLISHING ™

Written By
Grand Sheik Brother Kudjo Adwo El
Moorish Science Temple of America
Subordinate Temple #5 – Toronto
Canaanland

Edited By
Sister Tauheedah S. Najee-Ullah El
Moorish Science Temple Califa

"Watch My Prophecies."

© 2016, 2020
Califa Media ®
Lafayette, Indiana

Compiled by
Grand Sheik Kudjo Adwo El
Moorish Science Temple of America
Subordinate Temple #5 - Toronto
Canaanland

Edited by
Sister Tauheedah S. Najee-Ullah El
Moorish Science Temple Califa

ISBN-13: 978-1-952828-77-5

All Rights Reserved. Without Prejudice. No Part Of This Book May Be Reproduced Or Transmitted In Any Form By Any Means, Electronic, Photocopying, Mechanical, Recording, Information Storage Or Retrieval System Unless For The Liberation Of Min And Gaining Knowledge Of Self.

Califa Media®
A Moorish Guide Publishing Company
califamedia.com
All Rights, Remedies & Liberties Reserved

Table of Contents

Moorish American Prayer i

Introduction 1

Examination of Select Hadith and Prophesies of Noble Drew Ali .. 7

    8. 8
    14. 11
    17. 13
    24. 17
    28. 20
    31. 24
    32. 27
    33. 30
    37. 34
    40. 37
    50. 37
    53. 40
    62. 48
    72. 51
    73. 53
    91. 56
    98. 59
    99. 60
    102. 61
    103. 62
    107. 63
    130. 64
    137. 67
    139. 70
    141. 75
    150. 78
    172. 85
    178. 87
    181. 89
    185. 92
    186. 94
    208. 97
    236. 99
    242. 100
    248. 101
    251. 101
    254. 102
    267. 102

Other Predictions from the Prophet Noble Drew Ali 103

Notes 126

Other Titles Available from Califa Media® 127

Moorish American Prayer

ALLAH, the Father of the Universe, the Father of Love, Truth, Peace, Freedom and Justice. ALLAH is my protector, my guide, and my Salvation by night and by day, through His Holy Prophet DREW ALI.

Introduction

Noble Drew Ali, Prophet of the Moorish Americans and Universal Prophet of the Nations of the Earth has statements that were recorded by Moors that lived during and after the time of the Prophet's existence on the Earth plane. Although there were no audio recordings of his speeches, lectures or statements, we can look at society and the conditions that exist today, relate things in society to what Noble Drew Ali stated to see if he was legitimate and a true Prophet or a false Prophet. Noble Drew Ali was born Cherokee which lets us know that he was aboriginal and Indigenous to the Americas and did not come here on a slave ship or live a servant of colonial modern Europeans.

Among Native Americans, oral literature, still prevalent, enjoyed an exalted status in the nineteenth century. Those who performed stories, songs, and rituals were some of the most valued members of a community. Their performances served to remind the members of a community of their origin, how they came to be in a particular place, and how they should continue to live. Most native traditions distinguished between three oral genres: narrative, song, and ritual drama. In all these genres the oral tradition was informed by a central belief that human beings should strive for harmony with the universe.

Oral Tradition (n): a community's cultural and historical traditions passed down by word of mouth or example from one generation to another without written instruction.

oral (adj.): 1620s, from Late Latin oralis, from Latin os (genitive oris) "mouth, opening, face, entrance," from PIE *os- "mouth" (cognates: Sanskrit asan "mouth," asyam "mouth, opening," Avestan ah-, Hittite aish, Middle Irish a "mouth," Old Norse oss "mouth of a river," Old English or "beginning, origin, front").

statement (n.): 1775, "what is stated," from state (v.) + -ment. From 1789 as "action of stating;"

state (v.): 1590s, "to set in a position," from state (n.1); the sense of "declare in words" is first attested 1640s, from the notion of "placing" something on the record.

-ment: suffix forming nouns, originally from French and representing Latin -mentum, which was added to verb stems sometimes to represent the result or product of the action. French inserts an -e- between the verbal root and the suffix (as in commenc-e-ment from commenc-er; with verbs in ir, -i- is inserted instead (as in sent-i-ment from sentir). Used with English verb stems from 16c. (for example merriment, which also illustrates the habit of turning -y to -i- before this suffix).

prophecy (n.): c. 1200, prophecie, prophesie, "function of a prophet," from Old French profecie (12c. Modern French prophétie) and directly from Late Latin prophetia (source also of Spanish profecia, Italian profezia), from Greek propheteia "gift of interpreting the will of the gods," from prophetes (see prophet). Meaning "thing spoken or written by a prophet" is from c. 1300.

Prophet Noble Drew Ali made many statements that the average Asiatic in America would consider just words from a brother. The reality of Noble Drew Ali's words is that everything he says is spirit. So it would be wise to take heed to his words since he is a conduit for the wisdom of Allah to get to Spirit Man distorted by the murky ethers, flesh or the Physical Plane. When Moors speak highly of Noble Drew Ali it is due to his humanitarian perspective and wealth of knowledge, that when applied transforms the student as Man (which includes Wombman) from being his lower self to Man being his higher self and free from mental slavery. The words spoken by Noble Drew Ali are Prophetic at the same time divine Truth and instructions, or steps, tablets, dosage, a mental spiritual program to make his people, and the Nations better Citizens.

Many people doubt the messages in the Oral Statements from Noble Drew Ali and relate them to hearsay.

Hearsay (n.) "information communicated by another, gossip," mid-15c., from phrase to hear say (Middle English heren seien, Old English herdon secgan). The notion is "hear (some people) say;" from hear (v.) + say (v.). As an adjective from 1570s. Hearsay evidence (1670s) is that which the witness gives not from his own perception but what was told to him.

Heresy (n.) "doctrine or opinion at variance with established standards" (or, as Johnson defines it, "an opinion of private men different from that of the catholick and Orthodox Church"), c. 1200, from Old French heresie, eresie "heresy," and by extension "sodomy, immorality" (12c.), from Latin hæresis, "school of thought, philosophical sect." The Latin word is from Greek hairesis "a taking or choosing for oneself, a choice, a means of taking; a deliberate plan, purpose; philosophical sect, school," from haireisthai "take, seize," middle voice of hairein "to choose," a word of unknown origin, perhaps from PIE *ser- (5) "to seize" (source of Hittite šaru "booty," Welsh herw "booty").

The Greek word was used by Church writers in reference to various sects, schools, etc. in the New Testament: the Sadducees, the Pharisees, and even the Christians, as sects of Judaism. Hence the meaning "unorthodox religious sect or doctrine" in the Latin word as used by Christian writers in Late Latin. But in English bibles it usually is translated sect.

Heretic (n.) "one who holds a doctrine at variance with established or dominant standards," mid-14c., from Old French eretique (14c., Modern French hérétique), from Church Latin haereticus "of or belonging to a heresy," as a noun, "a heretic," from Greek hairetikos "able to choose" (in the New Testament, "heretical"), verbal adjective of hairein (see heresy).

Most do not deal with knowledge most cater to beliefs and illusions. To be a Mastermind it is utterly important to realize the power of faith. Faith in anything empowers. Someone homeless has faith that a little bit of light will shine. Then here comes Feed the Hungry giving out food and clothes packages. Faith.

Faith (n.) mid-13c., faith, feith, fei, fai "faithfulness to a trust or promise; loyalty to a person; honesty, truthfulness," from Anglo-French and Old French feid, foi "faith, belief, trust, confidence; pledge" (11c.), from Latin fides "trust, faith, confidence, reliance, credence, belief," from root of fidere "to trust," from PIE root *bheidh- "to trust" (source also of Greek pistis "faith, confidence, honesty;" see bid). For sense evolution, see belief. Accommodated to other English abstract nouns in -th (truth, health, etc.).

From early 14c. as "assent of the mind to the truth of a statement for which there is incomplete evidence," especially "belief in religious matters" (matched with hope and charity).

And faith is neither the submission of the reason, nor is it the acceptance, simply and absolutely upon testimony, of what reason cannot reach. Faith is: the being able to cleave to a power of goodness appealing to our higher and real self, not to our lower and apparent self. - Matthew Arnold, "Literature & Dogma," 1873

Noble Drew Ali knew that the state of mental slavery of Asiatics in North America was so deep that in order to free them he had to present the Universal Law and Natural Law Ancient principles and concepts in a way that anyone with mental slavery would understand (belief), so they can overstand (faith) and eventually innerstand (fruition).

CHAPTER VII

The Friendship of Jesus and Lamaas--Jesus Explains to Lamaas the Meaning of Truth

23. And Jesus said: "It is the consciousness that man is aught; that Allah and man are one;

24. That naught is naught; that power is but illusion; that heaven and earth and hell are not above, around, below, but in; which in the light of aught becomes the naught, and Allah is all."

25. Lamaas asked: "Pray, what is faith?"

26. And Jesus said: "Faith is the surety of the omnipotence of Allah and man; the certainty that man will reach the deific life.

27. Salvation is a ladder reaching from the heart of man to heart of Allah.

28. It has three steps; Belief is first, and this is what man thinks, perhaps, is truth.

29. And faith is next, and this is what man knows is truth.

30. Fruition is the last, and this is man himself, the truth.

31. Belief is lost in faith; and in fruition is lost; and man is saved when he has reached deific life; when he and Allah are one." – Holy Koran of the Moorish Science Temple of America.

By speaking prophetic to a mentally dead people it will cause them to have faith when prophesies manifest. A mentally dead people need Prophets. Do your research on Prophets and see how many come up. Some are false but the fact remains the same. Mentally dead people needs Prophets and a True and Divine Prophet to will lead the way with Love. Love is the first principle of the Moorish Americans and its relation to faith will allow all to receive the message from Allah/God/Creative Force etc through Noble Drew Ali's Oral Statements.

Rare is it that you find a real prophet whose mission is the salvation of the nations. The land is full of false prophets whose mission is to fleece the people.

The time was and now is that there should come into the land a prophet in the likeness of his brothers, to redeem them from sin and slavery. Truly this Prophet Noble Drew Ali is the man, bringing with him the message of Love, Truth, Peace, Freedom, and Justice, which alone can save the nations. Like the coming of Jesus, he does not come from the elect, nor the rich, nor the mighty in worldly power, but all power is given unto him to do good. This power is from Allah.

It will be his works that will make men of every nation accept the truth that he brings. It will be through his teachings that the nations of the earth will understand the will of the Master; it will be through him that "Peace on earth and good will to all men" shall come. It will be through his work that humanity will be brought from the slime of life and placed on the solid rock of salvation. – Savior of Humanity Moorish Literature / Moorish Guide Newspaper

The thousands of Moorish Americans will follow their leaders. Regardless of propaganda put forth by those who have designs to hinder them in the work for the advancement of their people. We will not stop to question the requisites, qualifications nor anything else, so long as our leaders who have investigated and passed on the course of action which we feel is enough endorsement for us to act.

We have long known that the first attempt to crush the leaders of any movement or organization is to plant descent ion among their followers. Such will never will never be the case with the Moorish Americans, for when we have chosen our leaders that within itself tells the world that we are going to follow them. All of the knocks and slams that come from anyone against our leaders will be ignored by us. Where they lead us we will follow. – Following Our Leaders Moorish Literature / Moorish Guide Newspaper

Examination of Select Hadith and Prophesies of Noble Drew Ali

8.

Bro. G. Cook-Bey, G.S. (Emeritus) of Temple 1, Chicago, Ill. said that the Holy Prophet said, "Look around, and where you see people; one day, wild animals will be roaming down the streets."

Danger in the Backyard
J.D. Heyman
People.com
July 12, 2004

Once upon a time—at 2 a.m. last Sept. 7, to be specific—Tim Foster woke with a start. Strange noises—loud thudding and grunting noises—emanated from the front room of his house in suburban Deep Creek Lake, Md. Foster, 43, scrambled out of bed and found a 252-lb. black bear "grabbing each side of our freezer and trying to yank it out the door," he says. Three bear cubs stood by, watching. Foster, who stands 6'8" and weighs 260 lbs., yelled and managed to drive the burglars down his driveway—until Mama Bear turned the tables. "She charged me. I got chased right back into the house," he says. The Fosters remained under siege in their own home until wildlife officials eventually sedated the intruder. "I enjoy looking at bears in the wild," says Foster, no longer traumatized. "I just don't want them on my back porch."

What to Do About Black Bears
Adapted from the book Wild Neighbors
Humane Society.org

As black bear numbers increase in some North American communities and more people move into bear habitat, encounters between bears and people have risen. Whether you live in bear country or are just visiting, you can take simple steps to avoid conflicts. Bears have acute eyesight and hearing. Their sense of smell is seven times greater than a bloodhound's. They have a keen ability to detect pet food, garbage, barbecue grills and bird feeders—and once they locate a food source, they remember where it is. Bears are normally wary of people, but if a bear finds food without getting frightened away, he may come back for more. Each time this happens, he can become less fearful—and this habituation can lead to problems. Conflicts can heighten during

hyperphagia, a feeding frenzy in late summer and fall in which bears bulk up for hibernation, gaining 3-4 pounds and consuming 20,000 calories a day.

Deer Heaven: How Suburbia Became the Animals' Ideal Habitat
By Liza Mundy
Washington Post
April 26, 2009

Though deer are becoming almost as ubiquitous in the suburbs as squirrels and rabbits, there is a great deal that biologists and wildlife managers don't know about how they dwell among us. "It's a weird place to find it," Ferebee says. Ferebee thought he knew this deer pretty well. In the past eight years, he has tracked five radio-collared does in all, and learned, among other things, that some spend more than half their time outside Rock Creek Park's boundaries. Their overall ranges vary: Some dwell within a quarter-mile radius, while others meander a bit farther, covering two miles. One doe pretty much lived in the neighborhoods around 16th Street NW, browsing in yards and bedding in gardens. Over time, two of Ferebee's does were hit by cars, and one--the yard-dweller--had to be euthanized because of an injury. Another slipped out of her collar. This doe is, or was, the only one with whom he remained in contact. When Ferebee first came to work in Rock Creek Park in 1991, it was a big deal to see even one white-tailed deer, the most common kind in North America. "You could go weeks without seeing one, and when you did see one, it was a significant thing," he says.

14.
Bro. J. Blakely-Bey said that the Holy Prophet said, "If the European be just, they would have an Asiatic Vice-President, and if they had an Asiatic President, they would have a European Vice-President."

Obama Chooses Biden as Running Mate
Adam Nagourney and Jeff Zeleny
August 23, 2008
New York Times

Senator Barack Obama has chosen Senator Joseph R. Biden Jr. of Delaware to be his running mate, turning to a leading authority on foreign policy and a longtime Washington hand to fill out the Democratic ticket, Mr. Obama announced in text and e-mail messages early Saturday.

Mr. Obama's selection ended a two-month search that was conducted almost entirely in secret. It reflected a critical strategic choice by Mr. Obama: To go with a running mate who could reassure voters about gaps in his résumé, rather than to pick someone who could deliver a state or reinforce Mr. Obama's message of change.

Mr. Biden is the chairman of the Senate Foreign Relations Committee, and is familiar with foreign leaders and diplomats around the world. Although he initially voted to authorize the war in Iraq — Mr. Obama opposed it from the start — Mr. Biden became a persistent critic of President George W. Bush's policies in Iraq.

17.
Sister M. Tiggs El of Temple 9 said that the Holy Prophet said, "When the Europeans go back to Europe, the climate would go back to what it used to be." (the climate in the United States at one time was a tropical climate before the Europeans came here).

WHAT IS THE "BACK TO EUROPE MOVEMENT?
back2europe.org/About-Us

It is an international ministry network in helping to develop a process of mobilizing the Church around the world to reach Europe with the gospel.

VISION
To motivate and assist the European and the Global Church to work together to see the Kingdom of God manifested in the Europe of today and of the future.

MISSION
To connect the different missionary forces with the needs of Europe, in order to show God's love through sharing the Good News, and engaging in discipleship, the growing and strengthening of God's people, the planting of churches and reaching the 'less reached'

Americans renouncing US citizenship soars to yet another record high...
Simon Black
sovereignman.com
October 27, 2015

1,426. That's the number of Americans who renounced their US citizenship last quarter according to the US government's report just released this morning. That's a record high for a single quarter, easily beating the last record high set earlier this year, which beat the previous record high set in 2013.

This is clearly a trend on the rise, and it certainly raises the question: why? What is it about the United States that drives so many citizens to leave? Two main reasons: The first group consists of people who just can't take it anymore. Constant warfare, intimidation, and the steady erosion of freedom have pushed

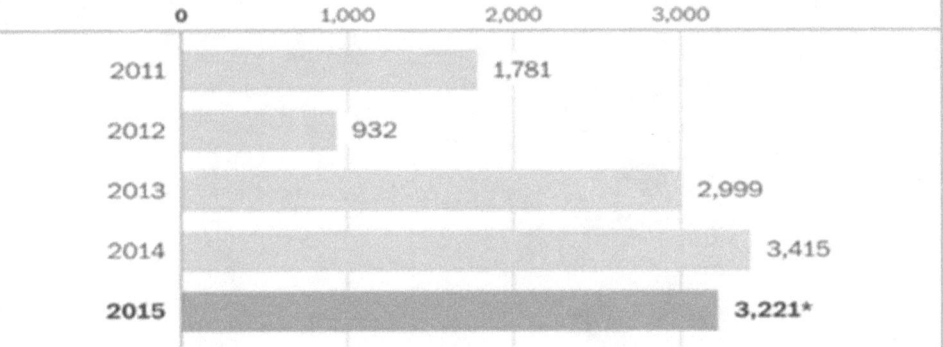

Annual Number of Expatriates

The U.S. government publishes the names of U.S. citizens who surrender their citizenship and long-term U.S. residents who do something similar. Most do so for tax purposes. These figures have grown in a marked way in recent years. When the federal government published figures for the third quarter of 2015 last week, this year's still incomplete tally came close to topping the figure reached over the course of 2014.

Year	Number
2011	1,781
2012	932
2013	2,999
2014	3,415
2015	3,221*

* Includes first, second and third quarter data. Fourth quarter not yet complete.

Source: U.S. Department of Treasury
THE WASHINGTON POST

them to their breaking points. They look around and think, "This is NOT the country that I grew up in." And they renounce their citizenship in protest of a government they no longer want to be associated with. But that's a small percentage of former citizens. For the vast majority of people who renounce their US citizenship, it ultimately comes down to a single issue: taxes. And there are three categories of tax-motivated renunciants.

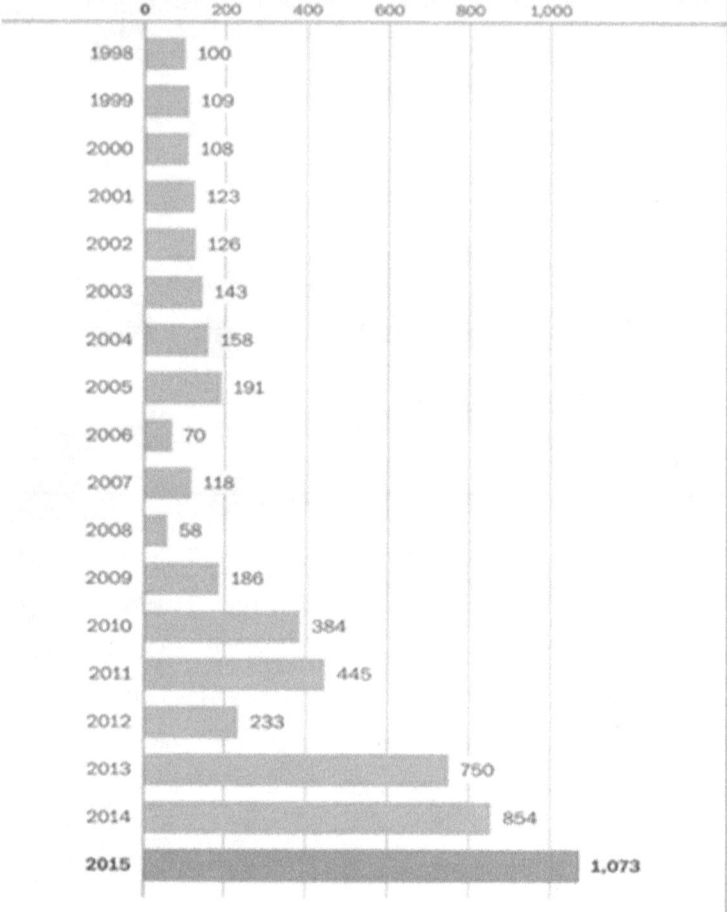

Quarterly Average Number of Expatriates

Each quarter, the U.S. government publishes the names of Americans who have decided to surrender their U.S. citizenship and long-term U.S. residents who have decided to do something similar. Most live abroad and do so to avoid U.S. taxes. But the share taking this step is growing, dramatically.

Year	Number
1998	100
1999	109
2000	108
2001	123
2002	126
2003	143
2004	158
2005	191
2006	70
2007	118
2008	58
2009	186
2010	384
2011	445
2012	233
2013	750
2014	854
2015	1,073

Source: U.S. Department of Treasury
THE WASHINGTON POST

24.
The Holy Prophet told the Moors that "one day you will go to the store, and there will be soldiers there with guns with bayonets on them, and they will not let you enter. They will order you to move on."

Detroit Race Riots 1943
Pbs.org

The Detroit riot began at a popular and integrated amusement park known as Belle Isle. On the muggy summer evening of June 20, 1943, the playground was ablaze with activity. Several incidents occurred that night including multiple fights between teenagers of both races. White teenagers were often aided by sailors who were stationed at the Naval Armory nearby. As people began leaving the island for home, major traffic jams and congestion at the ferry docks spurred more violence. On the bridge which led back to the mainland, a fight erupted between a total of 200 African Americans and white sailors. Soon, a crowd of 5,000 white residents gathered at the mainland entrance to the bridge ready to attack black vacationers wishing to cross. By midnight, a ragged and understaffed police force attempted to retain the situation, but the rioting had already spread too far into the city.

Two rumors circulated which exacerbated the conflict. At the Forest Club, a nightclub in Paradise Valley which catered to the black population, a man who identified himself as a police sergeant alerted the patrons that "whites" had thrown a black woman and her baby over the Belle Isle Bridge. The enraged patrons fled the club to retaliate. They looted and destroyed white-owned stores and indiscriminately attacked anyone with white skin. Similarly, white mobs had been stirred up by a rumor that a black man had raped and murdered a white woman on the bridge. The white mob centered around the downtown Roxy Theater which harbored a number of black movie-goers. As the patrons exited the theater, they found themselves surrounded by gangs who attacked and beat them. As rumors about the incidents in Paradise Valley and the downtown area spread through the night, so did the nature and the extent of the violence. White mobs targeted streetcars transporting black laborers to work, forced the cars to come to a halt, and attacked the passengers inside. They also targeted any cars with black owners, turning them over and setting them on fire.

By mid morning, black leaders in the community had asked Mayor Edward J. Jeffries to call in federal troops to quell the fighting. But it was not until late that evening, when white mobs invaded Paradise Valley, that Jeffries took the necessary steps to get outside help. Around midnight, a disturbing silence reigned over the city as a truce between the city's warring factions was kept by U.S. Army troops. More than 6,000 federal troops had been strategically stationed throughout the city. Detroit, under armed occupation, virtually shut down. The streets were deserted, the schools had been closed, and Governor Harry Francis Kelly had closed all places of public amusement. Most of the Paradise Valley community feared to leave their homes. Yet spurts of violence still flared up. As late as Wednesday, white mobs threatened black students leaving their graduation ceremony at Northeastern High School. The graduates had to be escorted home by truckloads of soldiers bearing bayonets.

28.
Bro. A. Wise-Bey, (Past) Grand Natl. Secretary said that the Holy Prophet said, "I didn't tell anyone where I was born at or who my parents were, because I didn't want people to make a shrine out of the place or make over my parents like was done with joseph and Mary."

Metaphysical Meaning of Joseph
Charles Fillmore
Metaphysical Bible Dictionary, 1931, 2013
Dover Publications

Joseph Meta. The state of consciousness in which we increase in character along all lines; we not only grow into a broader understanding but there is an increase of vitality and substance. Joseph is especially representative of the realm of forms. He was clothed with a coat of many colors; he was a dreamer and interpreter of dreams; the phenomenal was his field of action. Among the primal faculties of the mind Joseph represents imagination. This faculty has the power to throw onto the screen of visibility in substance and life forms every idea that the mind may conceive. While the imagination is a very necessary faculty and is powerful and productive, yet it is belittled and often derided and scorned by the other faculties of the mind while they are unawakened spiritually, while they are functioning in intellectual consciousness instead of true spiritual understanding (Joseph's brothers persecuted him).

Joseph in Egypt symbolizes the word of the imagination in subconsciousness, or the involution of a high spiritual idea. Joseph in Egypt could be said to represent also our highest perception of Truth, dealing with the realm of forms and bringing it into a more orderly state.

Joseph, our high ideal of Truth, comes down into the Egyptian darkness of sense consciousness, and under the law will finally raise it into spiritual light. In the process Joseph seems to die, but his "bones" remain. The substance of Truth is an abiding presence, though its form may be lost to sight.

Joseph and Mary, the parents of Jesus, represent wisdom and love, which have been ideas in mind but are now to bring forth a manifestation in substance (Luke 2:4, 5). Joseph might also be said to represent the Son of man and Mary the divine motherhood (Luke 2:40-52).

Mary Meta. The feminine, the soul, the affectional and emotional phase of man's being, both when seemingly bound and limited by sensate thought, and in its freed, exalted state.

Mary, the mother of Jesus, represents the soul that magnifies the Lord "daily in the temple" and through its devotions prepares itself for the higher life. She signifies the divine motherhood of love. She can also be said to be intuition.

Jesus, the perfected-man manifestation, is conceived in the intuitive or soul nature, and is molded in its substance. This coming of the Christ body into activity is the result of an exalted idea sown in the mind and matured by the soul (Mary). The soul is devout and expectant. It believes in the so-called miraculous as a possibility. Mary expected the birth of the Messiah, according to the promise of the Holy Spirit. She was overshadowed by that high idea; it formed in her mind the seed that quickened into the cell, and in due season there were aggregations of cells strong enough in their activity to attract the attention of the outer consciousness, and what is called the birth of Christ took place.

Mary, the soul, the mother of Jesus as mentioned in Luke 2:34, 35, refers to the conservative, conventional principle that suffers when the new order of life and law is set up. The soul has been bound by race tradition and custom until it is atrophied. Now it is coming to life, and in its travail it reveals the Lord's body.

Mary the mother of Jesus, Mary Magdalene, Mary of Bethany, Martha, and the other women who were with Jesus and His disciples so much during His ministry, "who ministered unto them of their substance," all represent phases of the individual soul.

A wonderful lesson of constancy, gratitude, love, faithful attachment, and service is set before us in the glimpses of Mary Magdalene that are given in the Gospels. Wherever she is mentioned the power of love, devotion, and service is revealed. Her whole life and all that she had were apparently dedicated to the Christ.

The soul consciousness in each individual is capable of the strongest, deepest, and fullest allegiance to Truth. It is constantly seeking something that will satisfy. It can never be happy or at peace until the feelings are redeemed and harmonized by the Holy Spirit, until God's presence is known, felt, and fully realized throughout the individual being. - Metaphysical Bible Dictionary

The Holy family depicted in a mural inside Castries Cathedral. Castries, Saint Lucia

31.

Sister M. Tiggs El and other Moors reported that the Holy Prophet said that "Chicago, Illinois is going to be our new Mecca."

5 Reasons Chicago is the Next Black Tech Mecca
Courtney Bell
Rolling Out.com
December 16, 2015

(Excuse the connotative language in this article)

Fabian Elliott is a hybrid entrepreneur. As founder and CEO of Black Tech Mecca Inc., he is leading his organization to transform Chicago into a "global Black tech mecca" through the development of a thriving Black tech ecosystem. Elliott shared with rolling out why he feels Chicago is the next Black technology mecca.

Chicago is a power city – Beyond just the Black and tech communities, Chicago is a major player on the global stage. It is the 3rd largest city in the US and ranked No. 7 in the world on the 2014 Global Cities Index 2014 (produced by A.T. Kearney). Chicago is also home to two of the world's most prestigious universities — the University of Chicago and Northwestern University.

There is a vibrant tech scene – The Windy City is very serious about technology. According to the Illinois Technology Association, Chicago is the top U.S. city for growth-stage technology companies. All of the generations of major tech giants have a presence in the city. Also, research reveals the number of jobs at tech companies in Chicago are growing at a rate that ranks the city sixth among the nation's top 20 tech markets.

The city has a clear vision – Chicago not only has a vision, but also a solid plan. The Chicago Technology Plan consists of 28 initiatives within five broad strategies. It enables the city to realize its vision of becoming a place where technology fuels opportunity, inclusion, engagement and innovation. Together, these five technology-focused strategies provide the path to solidifying Chicago a place as one of the world's leading cities.

There is a strong black nucleus – About 100 years ago, the Great Migration to Chicago was initiated by Robert Abbott and the Chicago Defender. This brought many Black people from the South to the city for opportunities fueled by the booming industries. This played a major role in Chicago growing to be the third largest urban Black population in the nation. Along with the sheer numbers, the city also has a history of Black influence and current direct connections to some of the most powerful Black people on the planet, including President Obama, Oprah Winfrey, and countless other power brokers.

There is a collaborative culture – Surprisingly enough, there is currently not a reigning "global Black tech mecca," so we are creating the very first one in Chicago. We are fortunate to have a special culture in the community that allows us to collaborate with key community partners such as [BlackinTech], Blue1647, Code2040, and many others.

32.
The Holy Prophet Noble Drew Ali told the Moors that "Chicago is doomed and Detroit must go down for what they have done to I, your Prophet", (the Holy Prophet was unjustly arrested in both Detroit, Michigan and Chicago, Illinois during His divine ministry.)

Chicago Violence: Weekend Shootings Push City to 400 Homicides This Year
Warner Todd Huston
Briebart.com
October 12, 2016

Coming off a September that was Chicago's most violent month in over a decade, the past weekend's toll of violence has pushed the Windy City's number of murders to over 400 thus far this year.

September's violence yielded 59 murders and 362 gunshot victims, marking the Democratic-run city's deadliest month since 2002, according to analysis by The Chicago Tribune.

September also witnessed a gruesome murder of a baby when the child's head was found floating in a lagoon in a city park.

As the Tribune reports, with October well underway, "at least 2,434 people have been shot in the city. That's 347 more than during the same period last year and 583 more than in 2013." The paper goes on to report that 404 people have been shot and killed thus far this year, 55 more than during the same period in 2013.

The weekend's most tragic shooting was the death of 3-year-old Eian Santiago, who was shot in the head by his 6-year-old brother while playing with his father's handgun, which the former gang member bought illegally.

The total level of Chicago violence year to date has reached 2,447 total shot with 416 total homicides (all causes included). - http://www.breitbart.com

---

In Detroit, Water Crisis Symbolizes Decline, and Hope
Bill Mitchell
National Geographic.com
August 2014

DETROIT—Rochelle McCaskill was in her bathroom about to rinse the soap off her hands when the water stopped. Slowed by lupus and other ailments, she made her way to a bedroom window, peered out, and spotted a guy fiddling with her water valve.

"There must be a mistake," she yelled down. McCaskill explained that she had just paid $80 on her $540.41 overdue bill, enough, she thought, to avoid a shutoff. The man wasn't interested in the details. He cranked off her water and marked the sidewalk by her valve with bright blue spray paint, a humiliation inflicted on delinquent customers that McCaskill likened to "a scarlet letter." Then he drove off in a truck with the red, white, and black logo dreaded citywide: "Detroit Water Collections Project."

Nearly 19,500 Detroiters have had their water service interrupted since March 1. The Water and Sewerage Department, under pressure to reduce more than $90 million in bad debt, ordered shutoffs for customers who owed at least $150 or had fallen at least two months behind on their bills. The decision to take such drastic measures, done with little warning, ignited a controversy that prompted protests and arrests, more bad publicity for the struggling city, global dismay, and a warning from the United Nations.

33.

Sister M. Howell-Bey of Temple 19, Flint, Michigan heard the Holy Prophet say, "One day, grass is going to grow up in Detroit." (Where there were once businesses and houses in Detroit. Michigan, there is grass growing in those locations now. The city of Detroit has gone down, and where there were businesses during the 1920's 193o's and 1940's, there are grassy fields now.)

Up Close: 8 Most Abandoned Neighborhoods in Detroit
Steve Neavling
Motor City Muckraker
June 6, 2014

Eight neighborhoods in Detroit have been so ravaged by crime, foreclosures, fires and scrappers that more than a third of the homes and businesses are abandoned, according to recently released findings from an unprecedented survey of every Detroit parcel.

Many of the areas have been consumed by thick brush, collapsing houses and discarded tires.

A quarter of the city's houses and buildings are vacant, according to the survey led by the Detroit Blight Removal Task Force and Motor City Mapping. Below is a ranking of neighborhoods with the highest percentage of vacant homes and buildings.

8. Brightmoor

% of unoccupied buildings: 34.2%

# of unoccupied buildings: 1,636

In the 1920s, Brightmoor was a neighborhood of modest homes for working-class immigrants and southerners who came to Detroit for auto jobs. But residential flight over the past five decades has turned some of the neighborhood into an urban prairie, making it an ideal location for small farms. The area, however, is rife with violent crime.

37.
Bro. J. Foster-Bey of Temple 4 and 25 heard the Holy Prophet say, "We (The Moors) are a hard-head, stiff-neck, mean set of people that have never did anything except at the point of a sword."

10 Lessons You Don't Want to Learn the Hard Way
G. Ann Wilkerson
Urban Cusp.com
May 21, 2012

Keep your personal business to yourself

Not everyone needs to know everything about you – not your friends, co-workers and certainly not the general public. Living in the social media driven culture in which we live, it has become habitual to publicize even the most private aspects of ourselves. But being so open leaves one very vulnerable to the scrutiny, misjudgment and potential mal-intentions of others. So, before you tell your co-workers about your wild weekend with the girls or change your relationship status on Facebook, just think, "Is this really everyone's business?"

Closed mouths don't get fed

Never be afraid to ask for or, when necessary, demand what you want and deserve. I've missed out on several opportunities simply because I never asked for consideration. Whether it's a promotion, a hot date or even a free meal, give yourself first consideration. Nine times out of ten – you deserve it.

Politics do matter

I hate playing games. And furthermore, I hate being fake or phony. But sometimes you have to be. Smile, shake hands, network and always be polite. I've made the mistake (more times than I'd like to admit) of making enemies out of people that in the long run, if I had just shown a little diplomacy, could have turned out to be bountiful resources or advocates. Even if you choose not to play the game, at least learn the rules. You may not end up sweeping the board, but the last thing you want to do is get stuck because you pissed off the wrong person.

Sometimes, it is important to burn bridges

Yes, everyone has value. But not everyone deserves your time or energy. This applies to all relationships – romantic and platonic. Some people are just baggage, negative baggage at that, weighing you down. So, if you have a long time "friend" that wants the goods but won't commit or a girlfriend that you know gossips about you behind your back, let them go. Burn the bridge and feel the release of the dead weight.

You can learn to live on a lot less than you think

The term "poor" is most certainly relative. I have experienced several episodes of "poverty" throughout my life. Each time I thought I couldn't make it through. Yet, I always made it through unscathed and, in most cases, triumphant. Poverty is relative, but so is wealth. Don't let your desire for a certain income prevent you from making decisions that may leave you rich in life experience or happiness.

Your degree will only get you so far

Most college students have this romanticized outlook on life after college. They believe that armed with this magical piece of paper, the doors will just fly open and employers will come chasing after them. Poor things.

40.
Bro. I. Cook-Bey, G.G. (Emeritus) of Ill, said that the Holy Prophet Noble Drew Ali told the Moors that "the Europeans went to the Moroccan government, and asked for permission to come over here (to the United states) to develop this land, and they were given a 50 year mandate to do so. Then the Europeans went to an old Sheik and asked him to give them some people to help them to develop this land. The Sheik told them to take those Moors, because they are not going to do anything."

50.
Bro, J. Foster-Bey of Temple 4 and 25 said that he heard the Holy Prophet say "People left the Garden of Eden, and died by the thousands, but it was the Moors that were able to traverse the desert, go into other parts of the world to inhabit."

The Blue Men of the Desert: A Legendary Culture
Rain for the Sahel and Sahara

Legendary herders and caravaners of the Sahara desert, the Tuareg are among the last nomads on earth. Their ancient written language, Tifinagh (or Tamasheq), their music, dance and culture have been the subject of fascinated study and speculation by generations of explorers, archaeologists and scholars. Tifinagh is thought to have derived from the ancient Berber script. The word Tifinagh means 'the Phoenician letters," or possibly comes from the Greek word for writing tablet, pínaks. It is not taught in schools, but is still used occasionally by the Tuareg for private notes, love letters and in decoration.

"Men and women towards each other are for the eyes and the heart, and not only for the bed."

Tuareg people have a long tradition of music and poetry. Many of the songs sing the praises of women. At festivals and gatherings, women clap and sing together in drum circles a matrilineal society, the Tuareg trace their families through women. For example, men hold political power, but when a chief dies, the title goes to his sister's son. In each family, it is the wife who owns the portable family home. She has her own herd of goats, sheep and camels – affording her financial independence should her husband leave her through death or divorce.

The camel is the primary mode of transportation for Tuareg men, and is a badge of joy and pride. Each year, Tuareg men engage in camel races at the annual Cure Salee (Salt Cure) festival in Ingall. Women prefer donkeys for their transport, and children also use donkeys to fetch water. Men are the sole creators of the famous Tuareg jewelry, while women work in straw and leather. Tuareg men cover their heads and mouths, to protect from dust and wind as well as observing respect for the power of the spoken word. Modesty in speech, manner and dress is expressed in both genders; however, women are not expected to veil themselves as the men.

For thousands of years, the Tuareg economy revolved around trans-Saharan trade. There are basically five trade routes that extend across the Sahara from the northern Mediterranean coast to the African cities on the southern edge of the desert. Tuareg merchants were responsible for bringing goods from these cities to the north. From there, they were distributed throughout the world. Because of the nature of transport and the limited space available in caravans, Tuareg usually traded in luxury items, which took up little space and on which a large profit could be made. Tuareg were also responsible for bringing enslaved people north from West Africa to be sold to Europeans and Middle Easterners. Many Tuareg settled into the communities with which they traded, serving as local merchants and representatives for their nomadic relations.

53.
Bro. J. Foster-Bey of Temple 4 and 25 said that the Holy Prophet said, "Before the End of Time, every knee will bow to Islam."

Dr. Mehmet Oz, host of "The Dr Oz Show" and vice chair and professor of surgery at Columbia University, was born in Ohio to Turkish parents. His mother's family was fiercely secular, while his father's family treated Islam as much more central to their lives. Dr. Oz has said he has struggled with his religious understanding but describes his beliefs as a mystical form of Islam closely related to Sufism.

57.

Sister A. Brown H of Temple 4 and 25 said that the Holy Prophet told the Moors, "Watch the newspapers and listen to the radio, I am going to make the European tell the truth."

The Ali Shuffle
Peter Moon
The Montauk Book of the Dead, 2005

At the current time, the door to Moorish mysteries is opening far and wide. The Age of Pisces is at an end, and the Moors are coming to receive their inheritance. Drew Ali instigated this process when he returned to America and released a publication known as the Circle Seven Koran. While Drew Ali did not deliver the concise formula as was clearly delineated in Synchronicity and the Seventh Seal, he represented the energy and was the energy of such. Drew Ali was very much a part of the mythos and reality that enabled me to write that book. What Drew Ali wrote was geared towards a format that would be accepted by his people at that particular time. It apparently worked quite well.

When the Moorish Science reached its peak in 1929, it was on the heels of one of the greatest, but most dangerous, discoveries Drew Ali ever made. In 1928, Ali attended a Pan American conference in Havana Cuba where he enjoyed broad recognition from a host of other countries. They were, of course, recognizing his sovereign status as a Moorish national who was representing the ancient empire of Amexem. Keep in mind that other countries had no reason to fear Drew Ali or what he represented. It was at this conference, however, that he received a document which was to change the face of Moorish Science forever and would eventually lead to what is known as the Great Schism. That is the name the Moorish community uses to refer to the dispersal of Moorish Science into different groups.

The document Drew Ali received was a copy of a mandate whereby the Amexem Empire extended a land grant of the entire Western Hemisphere to certain Europeans. I have not yet seen the document, and its exact contents are highly mysterious, yet its ramifications literally turned the United States of America upside down. Essentially, it "leased" America to a certain party for a particular number of years, not unlike the way China leased Hong Kong to Great Britain, The lease was up in 2004.

It is entirely reasonable to believe that such a document, if it still exists and can be brought to light, is a mere relic of a long forgotten era that has no significant meaning in today's legal system. That would be fine except for one very important point. If you have truly studied the detailed legal history of the United States of America, you would understand that there is more than a little truth to the prospect of their being such a document. Why? The entire legal history of the United States is predicated on such a proposition.

What is known is that Secretary of State Hughes, from the U.S. Government, attended the Pan American conference and was made privy to this mandate. So were several other heads of state. As a result, a closed-door conference between several nations was held in Geneva, Switzerland and a labyrinthine series of discussions and negotiations began. The Geneva conferences went on for some five years, but records are still kept sealed to this very day. It is known that several international banks called in their loans as a result of this potential legal threat and the stock market crashed in 1929.

About Richard Smith
UFO Teacher.com

European Confessions of a Moorish Legacy, has served as a spearhead of hot button paranormal discussion, circulating like wildfire in DVD format ever since its original presentation in Philadelphia at Temple University's Pan-African

It is not prejudice if it is a fact. I suggest reexamining one's position on this and accept the reality. Conveniently labeling truth as 'prejudice' is yet another heinous form of censorship and the ultimate form of ignorance and propaganda via the politics of fear.

Studies Community Education Program in 2007. Working with media host Curtis Davis, Smith produced a comprehensive six-part radio series on Occult Science Radio in 2012, expanding on his earlier lecture at Temple University.

62.

The Holy Prophet said. "One day, bombs are going to fall so that they won't miss a spot as wide as my shoe." He said that you are going to need a basement to hide in.

Air Force Rolls Out "Smarter" Smart Bombs
Cnn.com
October 18, 1996

WASHINGTON (CNN) -- The U.S. Air Force Thursday made public the results of tests done on a new generation of "smart bombs" that sail to their targets while being guided by the Global Positioning Satellite (GPS) system.

The bombs are the first non-nuclear weapons designed for use by the delta-winged B-2 Stealth Bomber, which has been largely without a mission since the end of the Cold War.

Sixteen of the precise 2,000 pound bombs were dropped on dummy targets at a Nevada desert test range on October 8th. They were dropped by three of the giant bombers flown from Whiteman Air Force Base in Missouri.

A press conference was held at the Pentagon to demonstrate for the news media the accuracy of the new weapons, known as the GPS-Aided Targeting System (GATS)/GPS Aided Munition (GAM).

Video tapes of the test run show that the bombs were accurate to within 20 feet of their targets after being dropped from 41,000 feet at a distance of more than six miles from a Stealth Bomber. The bombs can function in any weather because of their GPS guidance systems. Other "smart bombs" depend on laser guidance systems that can be adversely affected by clouds and foul weather.

The video tape of the test shows the bombs destroying rows of 8 by 20 foot "trailers" spread out across the desert with remarkable accuracy.

The once top secret B-2 "Spirit" was first shown to the public in 1988 but has never been used by the United States for anything other than air shows.

Originally designed to carry nuclear weapons into hostile territory without being detected by enemy radar, the end of the cold war left the $2 Billion plane virtually without a role.

Critics have called the B-2 program a $44 billion waste of taxpayer money, but the plane still has strong support on Capitol Hill.

Proponents of the plane argue that its stealth capability allow it to operate without the large number of support aircraft that other heavy bombers require such as radar jamming planes, fighter aircraft for protection and all the inflight refueling planes that are needed to keep those planes aloft.

The next batch of B-2's would come in at a cost of about $600 million per copy.

India set to acquire precision bomb technology
Gulshan Luthra
India Strategic
July 2007

Paris. Precision bombing with maximum impact and minimal collateral damage is the key to warfare now and later.

This is a requirement now from many angles, thanks to the emergence of urban terrorism from religious fanatics on a large scale all over the world.

While terrorists are legitimate targets, people near them are not. If they suffer in the process of attacks, many of them turn on the side of terrorists.

Legally, that also violates human rights, and today, no wing of the armed forces really wants to do that. Former Chief of Air Staff S P Tyagi is in fact on record as having said that the Indian Air Force's entire effort is now focused on all-weather precision engagement wherever required, and to minimize any collateral damage if that has to happen at all.

His predecessor, Air Chief Marshal S Krishnaswamy, had also made similar observations.

It's no surprise then that the state run Ordnance Factory Board (OFB) is negotiating the acquisition of all-weather precision bomb technology from US arms major Raytheon. Ben Ford, senior manager of Raytheon Missile Systems, told India Strategic at the Paris Air Show that Raytheon was in discussions with OFB to transfer the technology for the Enhanced Paveway-II Dual Mode GPS/Laser Guided Bombs for their indigenous manufacture in India.

The bombs will be used by the Indian Air Force (IAF) in a contingency.

Procedural **clearance** from the **US government** should be available, Ford added.

72.
Bro. J. Blakely-Bey said that the Holy Prophet said, "There is going to be an earthquake that will split the United States in two."

Two of the Most Dangerous Fault Lines in the U.S. May Be CONNECTED in California - And Scientist Warns They Will Cause a Catastrophic Earthquake if They Rupture Together

Wills Robinson
Dailymail.com
January 4, 2016

Two of the most dangerous fault lines in the United States could be connected below California and will cause a catastrophic earthquake if they rupture together, a scientist has warned.

The Hayward Fault, the most populated in the world, and the Rodgers Creek Fault are believed to be linked underneath the San Pablo Bay.

Their connection has been debated for years but, as a result of the discovery, residents have been warned to brace themselves because the results would be devastating if they were to crack together.

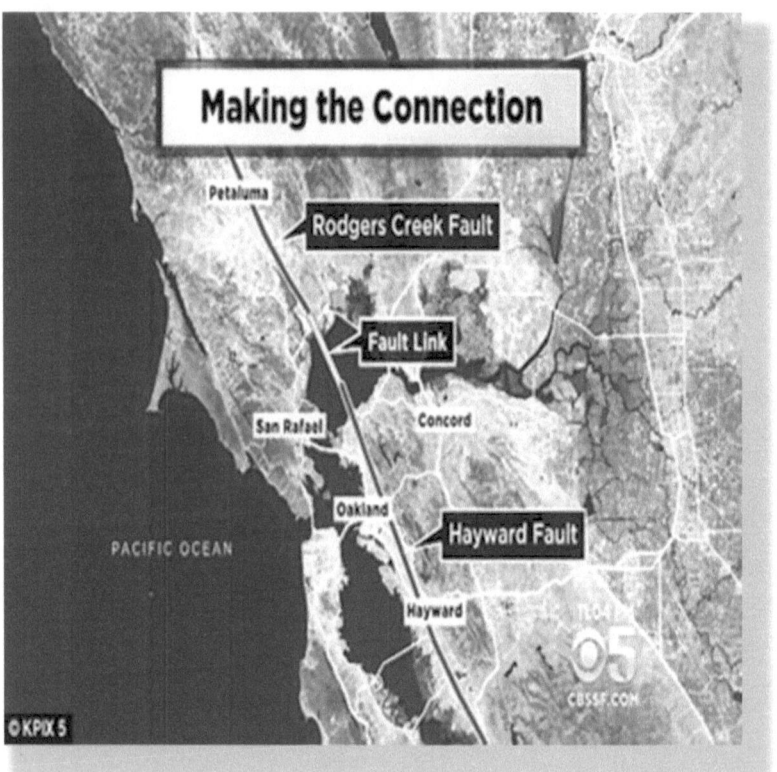

73.
Bro. E. Thomas El of Temple 4 and 43 said that the Holy Prophet said, "One day, 50 pound hail stones are going to fall."

World's Largest Hailstones
Hailstorms and Hailstone Size in the U.S.A.

Costliest

There have been a handful of hailstorms that resulted in $1 billion or more in damages in the U.S. The costliest storm appears to be that of April 10, 2001 which cut a swath along the I-70 corridor from eastern Kansas to southwestern Illinois and pounded the St. Louis area. Property damage was in excess of $2.4 billion in 2010 dollars. The hailstorm that struck the Dallas/Ft. Worth, Texas metro area on May 5, 1995 also caused an estimated $2 billion in damage (adjusted to current dollars). The only other $1 billion dollar hailstorm on record was that which pummeled the Front Range of Colorado between Colorado Springs and Fort Collins on July 11, 1990 causing $1.6 billion damage in 2010 inflation-adjusted dollars.

Deadliest

In spite of the enormous crop and property damage that hailstorms have caused only three people have ever been killed by falling hailstones in the United States: 1) a farmer caught in his field near Lubbock, Texas on May 13, 1930 2) a baby struck by large hail in Fort Collins, Colorado on July 31, 1979, and 3) a boater on Lake Worth, Texas on March 29, 2000.

Largest Stones

Mr. and Ms. Clarence Costner proudly display baseball-sized hail that fell on their farm near Norbonne, Missouri date unknown. The largest officially recognized hailstone on record to have been 'captured' in the U.S. was that which fell near Vivian, South Dakota last summer (2010) on July 23rd. It measured 8.0" in diameter, 18 ½" in circumference, and weighed in at 1.9375 pounds. Mr. Lee Scott, who collected, the monster stone originally planned to make daiquiris out of the hailstone but fortunately thought better and placed it in a freezer before turning it over to the National Weather Service for certification.

Other instances of 8-inch hail have been reported in the past but not certified. The U.S. Weather Bureau's Climatological Data by Sections Vol. 22, Part 2 April-June, 1935 mentions a hailstorm producing 8-inch diameter hailstones at Ponca City, Oklahoma on April 17, 1935.

STATE HAIL RECORDS

OFFICIAL

STATE	HAIL SIZE	LOCATION	DATE
KANSAS	7.75"	Wichita	Sept. 15, 2010
MINNESOTA	6.0"	Edgerton	July 4, 1968
	6.0"	Reading	July 28, 1986
NEBRASKA	7.0"	Aurora	June 22, 2003
*SOUTH DAKOTA	8.0"	Vivian	July 23, 2010
VERMONT	3.3"	Westford	July 16, 2009
WISCONSIN	5.7"	Wausau	May 1921

*Official USA record

UNOFFICIAL

STATE	HAIL SIZE	LOCATION	DATE
ALASKA	1.5"	Talkeetna	June 15, 2005
CALIFORNIA	2.5"	Salinas	Sept. 21, 1916
COLORADO	5.0"	Fort Collins	July 31, 1979
CONNECTICUT	2.5"	Hamden	July 10, 1989
D.C.	4.15"		May 26, 1953
FLORIDA	4.5"	Polk County	March 30, 1995
GEORGIA	4.25"	Hogansville	April 19, 2006
ILLINOIS	7.5"	Aurora	May 1, 1933
INDIANA	4.5"	Cayuga	May 5, 2000
IOWA	5.5"	Dubuque	June 16, 1882
KENTUCKY	5.0"	Princeton	April 3, 1974
OHIO	4.0"	Martins Ferry	June 5, 1933
MAINE	4.0"	Cumberland County	June 1, 1986
MARYLAND	4.0"	Annapolis	June 22, 1915
MICHIGAN	4.0"	Stony Point	March 27, 1991
MISSISSIPPI	4.0"	Batesville	April 27, 2011
MISSOURI	6.0"	Nodaway County	Sept. 5, 1898
NEW JERSEY	2.5"	Perth Amboy	June 23, 1906
NEW YORK	4.0"	Otsego County	Aug. 16, 1951
PENNSYLVANIA	5.5"	Meadville	June 26, 1950
OKLAHOMA	8.0"	Ponca City	April 17, 1935
SOUTH CAROLINA	4.25"	Turbeville	April 16, 2011
TENNESSEE	4.25"	Rogersville	April 9, 2011
TEXAS	6.0-8.0"	Gay Hill	Dec. 6, 1892
	6.0"	San Antonio	May 1946
UTAH	3.5"	Coalville	July 21, 1987
VIRGINIA	4.5"	Saltville	April 27, 2011

Source:
https://www.wunderground.com/blog/weatherhistorian/worlds-largest-hailstones

91.
Sister M. Payton-Bey said that the Holy Prophet said, "The biggest fool is the educated fool."

Anti-Intellectualism and the "Dumbing Down" of America
Ray Williams
Psychology Today Online
July 7, 2014

Susan Jacoby, author of The Age of American Unreason, says in an article in the Washington Post, "Dumbness, to paraphrase the late senator Daniel Patrick Moynihan, has been steadily defined downward for several decades, by a combination of heretofore irresistible forces. These include the triumph of video culture over print culture; a disjunction between Americans' rising level of formal education and their shaky grasp of basic geography, science and history; and the fusion of anti-rationalism with anti-intellectualism."

Mark Bauerlein, in his book, The Dumbest Generation, reveals how a whole generation of youth is being dumbed down by their aversion to reading anything of substance and their addiction to digital "crap" via social media.

Journalist Charles Pierce, author of Idiot America, adds another perspective: "The rise of idiot America today represents--for profit mainly, but also and more cynically, for political advantage in the pursuit of power--the breakdown of a consensus that the pursuit of knowledge is a good. It also represents the ascendancy of the notion that the people whom we should trust the least are the people who best know what they are talking about. In the new media age, everybody is an expert."

John W. Traphagan, Professor of Religious Studies at the University of Texas, argues the problem is that Asian countries have core cultural values that are more akin to a cult of intelligence and education than a cult of ignorance and anti-intellectualism. In Japan, for example, teachers are held in high esteem and normally viewed as among the most important members of a community. There is suspicion and even disdain for the work of teachers that occurs in the U.S. Teachers in Japan typically are paid significantly more than their peers in the U.S. The profession of teaching is one that is seen as being of central value in Japanese society and those who choose that profession are well compensated in terms of salary, pension, and respect for their knowledge and their efforts on behalf of children.

Bill Keller, writing in the New York Times argues that the anti-intellectual elitism is not an elitism of wisdom, education, experience or knowledge. The new elite are the angry social media posters, those who can shout loudest and more often, a clique of bullies and malcontents baying together like dogs cornering a fox. Too often it's a combined elite of the anti-intellectuals and the conspiracy followers – not those who can voice the most cogent, most coherent response. Together they foment a rabid culture of anti-rationalism where every fact is suspect; every shadow holds a secret conspiracy. Rational thought is the enemy. Critical thinking is the devil's tool.

98.

Bro. Smith-Bey of Temple 3 and 9 state that some Asiatics paid some hit-men (killers) to kill the Holy Prophet. When the hit-men went to the temple, where the Holy Prophet was teaching, that they opened the door, and found the temple building full of soldiers. The hit-men went back to the people that hired them, and told them, "don't you pay us to do anything to any of those Moorish-Americans." (During the life of the Holy Prophet there were many members of the National Guard, both officers and enlisted men that were members of the Moorish Science Temple of America in Chicago, Illinois.

99.
Bro. T. Booker-Bey, G.N.T. (Emeritus) said that the Holy Prophet gave a party for the Moors, and that the Prophet had everything fixed up nice. He even had pool tables for their enjoyment. The Moors were happy, and the Holy Prophet said, "I am happy, when my Moors are happy." But some unconscious Asiatics tried to break up the party. When they tried, some of the Moors, who were members of the National Guard, went to the Armory, and came back to the party with army tanks, trucks, and guns. When the Asiatics saw this, they took off with such fright that some of them ran into buildings, and knocked themselves out. He said that the word got out, "Don't mess with Prophet Noble Drew Ali, because He is connected with the government."

102.

Bro. T. Booker-Bey. G.N.T. (Emeritus) said that he was walking down the street in Chicago. Illinois, and an Arabian came out of a store, and asked him to come into the store. He went with him. The Arabian pointed at a man, and asked him. "Do you know who this is?" Bro. Booker-Bey said, "That is my Prophet." The Holy Prophet said, "all right son". The store was full of Arabians, and Bro. T. Booker-Bey said that all of them had Nationality Cards for the Moorish Science Temple of America.

103.
Moors that were in the Temple during the lifetime of the Holy Prophet Noble Drew Ali said that when the Holy Prophet came to town, you would have to go to the temple early to get a seat, and you could not get a seat in the front row because the foreign Moslems would be sitting in the front row to see and hear the Holy Prophet.

107.

Bro. O. Payton-Bey of Temple 4 and 25 said that the Holy Prophet said, "There are going to be new Moors that are going to come in with their eyes wide open, seeing and knowing, that are going to take you old Moors, seat you in the back, and carry out my law." (He was talking about new members of the Moorish Science Temple of America that would come into the Temple with their eyes wide open, seeing and knowing, and who would carry out the Holy Prophet's law).

130.
Bro. E. Thomas El said that the Holy Prophet said, "All nations will turn against the United States, one day."

Lawsuit Against The United States For Financial Damages

On May 5, 2000, a judgment was issued in a Havana court regarding the financial damages resulting from the U.S. blockade on Cuba.

Andrés Zaldívar Diéguez
May 15, 2015
Gramma.org.cu

ON May 5, 2000, the Civil and Administrative Court of Law at the Havana Provincial People's Court rendered Judgment no.47 on Civil Case number 1, pursuant to the lawsuit of the People of Cuba vs. the Government of the United States, for financial damages inflicted on Cuba, filed by the country's social and mass organizations.

In an assessment of the factors that make up the framework of this criminal economic war, experts and witnesses presented evidence – February 28 through March 10 – with compelling statements which demonstrated the responsibility of the U.S. government for systematic actions against Cuba in order to alienate public support for the Revolution, and thus destroy it.

The aggressive policy and its criminal effects on all economic sectors and the social life of the country were placed under scrutiny. As a result, the illegality of the blockade – indeed an act of genocide – in the light of international law was demonstrated, as well as the obligation of the U.S. government to atone for the harm caused by its immoral and illegal conduct, and to pay compensation for the damages caused.

Experts and witnesses demonstrated that since the beginning of the 60s, U.S. government measures against Cuba implied the loss of markets for its exports, as well as its main suppliers, as 70% of trade was previously conducted with the country. In industrial sectors, huge investments for the conversion of production technology were required, with the most adverse effects seen on vital production lines.

The negative financial effect caused by the distance of markets the island was obliged to turn to, in order to acquire all products (including medicines or the raw materials for their manufacture), with the consequent supply interruptions, the need to maintain large stocks and problems of transportation and operations, were all outlined.

The blockade measures attempted to prevent all maritime trade with Cuba. The banning from U.S. ports of ships of any nationality which traded with Cuba was imposed, and in force for 14 years, and after a brief period in which this policy was discontinued, the Torricelli Act in 1992 resumed it, resulting in the rising cost of freight and other damages. The evidence demonstrated the economic losses due to the ban on travel to Cuba by U.S. citizens; the refusal to allow Cuban aircraft to offer commercial flights to the United States, the inability to use the shortest routes to arrive at certain destinations, the resulting additional layovers and necessary use of technologically outdated equipment, together with many other adverse effects.

137.
Bro. J. Blakely-Bey said that the Holy Prophet said that "we are going to be taxed to death."

9 Things The Rich Don't Want You To Know About Taxes
David Cay Johnston
Willamette Weekly
April 12, 2011

3. In fact, the wealthy are paying less taxes.

The Internal Revenue Service issues an annual report on the 400 highest income-tax payers. In 1961, there were 398 taxpayers who made $1 million or more, so I compared their income tax burdens from that year to 2007.

Despite skyrocketing incomes, the federal tax burden on the richest 400 has been slashed, thanks to a variety of loopholes, allowable deductions and other tools. The actual share of their income paid in taxes, according to the IRS, is 16.6 percent. Adding payroll taxes barely nudges that number.

Compare that to the vast majority of Americans, whose share of their income going to federal taxes increased from 13.1 percent in 1961 to 22.5 percent in 2007.

Many of the very richest pay no current income taxes at all.

John Paulson, the most successful hedge-fund manager of all, bet against the mortgage market one year and then bet with Glenn Beck in the gold market the next. Paulson made himself $9 billion in fees in just two years. His current tax bill on that $9 billion? Zero.

Congress lets hedge-fund managers earn all they can now and pay their taxes years from now.

In 2007, Congress debated whether hedge-fund managers should pay the top tax rate that applies to wages, bonuses and other compensation for their labors, which is 35 percent. That tax rate starts at about $300,000 of taxable income— not even pocket change to Paulson, but almost 12 years of gross pay to the median-wage worker.

The Republicans and a key Democrat, Sen. Charles Schumer of New York, fought to keep the tax rate on hedge-fund managers at 15 percent, arguing that the profits from hedge funds should be considered capital gains, not ordinary income, which got a lot of attention in the news.

What the news media missed is that hedge-fund managers don't even pay 15 percent. At least, not currently. So long as they leave their money, known as "carried interest," in the hedge fund, their taxes are deferred. They only pay taxes when they cash out, which could be decades from now for younger managers. How do these hedge-fund managers get money in the meantime? By borrowing against the carried interest, often at absurdly low rates—currently about 2 percent.

Lots of other people live tax-free, too. I have Donald Trump's tax records for four years early in his career. He paid no taxes for two of those years. Big real-estate investors enjoy tax-free living under a 1993 law President Clinton signed. It lets "professional" real-estate investors use paper losses like depreciation on their buildings against any cash income, even if they end up with negative incomes like Trump.

139.
J. Blakely Bey told the Moors that the Holy Prophet said, "If you are not careful, your own brothers will try to put you in slavery."

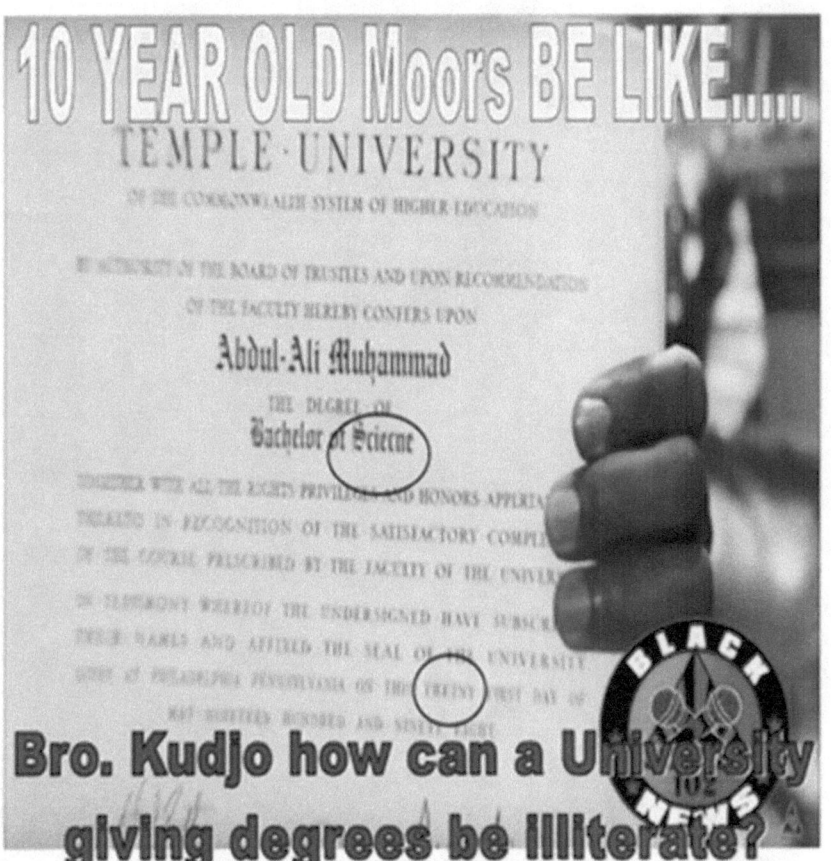

Dirty Moors be like..

Noble Drew Ali brought this flag!!!

141.

Sister A. Brown El of Temple 4 and 25 said that the Holy Prophet said, "One day, some of you Moors are going to be walking around with skippers (those are maggots) falling out of you, praying to die, and won't be able to die."

Eaten alive by maggots!
Occasionally stories surface about people being eaten by maggots. Just another internet hoax. Or is it?
February 28, 2011
Olivia Rose-Innes
Health24

Make sure it doesn't happen to you

If you're travelling to an area where parasitic maggots occur, this nasty problem (and others) can be prevented as follows:

- Maintain good personal hygiene
- Avoid soil likely to be contaminated by human excreta
- Wash and dry clothes thoroughly, and iron them if they've been hung outside
- Don't go barefoot
- Avoid insect bites
- Keep wounds clean and covered
- Keep food covered
- See your doctor if you've recently returned from endemic areas and you notice any unusual or persistent skin sores, itching or pain.
- And finally – always take any medical information you read on the 'net with a large pinch of salt, unless you find it on a highly reputable health site, like this one.

Opportunistic flesh-eaters

Myiasis can also occur when a fly (sometimes even the humble housefly) deposits larvae in a wound or decaying flesh (e.g. in cases of gangrene). Some species of larvae remain within the decaying tissue, and this can even be useful in keeping the wound clean. Other species, though – called "opportunistic" – like the screwworm, mainly found in central and South America, enter the surrounding living tissue and can even burrow internally.

Accidental flesh-eaters

Very occasionally, myiasis happens by accident. Maggots can find their way into the human body when they are swallowed in contaminated food, or when they come into contact with the urogenital tract in cases of poor hygiene (flies are attracted by the smell of faeces and urine).

Opportunistic and accidental myiasis scenarios are rare, and generally occur where invalids have neglected wounds and otherwise poor hygiene. Myiasis in such cases can be easily prevented by decent basic health care and keeping the immediate environment clean and free from flies. And if you do happen to eat a maggot, the chances are slim that the poor thing is going to survive your teeth and digestive juices.

150.

Bro. T. Booker-Bey, G.N.T. (Emeritus) said that the Holy Prophet told the Moors, "In two weeks, I am going down South. When I get down there, the Ku Klux Klan is going to stop me. At first, it is going to look like they are against me. Then they are going to lead me where I am going." The Holy Prophet made the trip, and things happened the way that he said that they would happen.

The NOI and KKK Alliance
Bruce Perry
"Malcolm X: The Last Speeches"
Pathfinder Press 1989

pp. 121-122

Yes, he's immoral [Elijah Muhammad]. You can't take nine teenaged women and seduce them and give them babies and not tell me you're—and then tell me you're moral. You could do it if you admitted you did it and admitted that the babies were yours. I'd shake your hand and call you a man. A good one too. Any time you seduce teenaged girls and make them be charged with adultery, make them hide your crimes, why, you're not even a man, much less a divine man. So, and this is what he did. He took at least nine that we know about. And I'm not speculating, because he told this to me himself. Yes, that's why he wants me dead because he knew as soon as I walked out that I'd tell it. Nine of them. Not two of them who are suing him, but nine of them. And the FBI knows it. The law in Chicago knows it. The press even knows it. And they don't expose the man.

And don't let me get out of here tonight without telling you why they won't expose him. Why they're afraid to expose him. They know that if they expose him, that he has them all set. See, the Black Muslim movement, it was organized in such a way that it attracted the most militant, the most uncompromising, the most fearless, and the youngest of the Black people in the United States. That's who went into it. Those who didn't mind dying. They didn't mind making a sacrifice. All they were interested in was freedom and justice and equality, and they would do anything to see that it was brought about. These are the people who have followed him for the past twelve years. And the government knows it. But all these upfront militants have been held in check by an organization that doesn't take an active part in anything. And therefore it cannot be a threat to anybody because it's not going to do anything against anybody but itself.

Don't you know? The way they threw that bomb in there they could have thrown it in a Ku Klux Klan house. Why do they want to bomb my house? Why don't they bomb the Klan? I'm going to tell you why.

In 1960, in December, in December of 1960, I was in the home of Jeremiah, the minister in Atlanta, Georgia. I'm ashamed to say it, but I'm going to tell you the truth. I sat at the table myself with the heads of the Ku Klux Klan. I sat there myself, with the heads of the Ku Klux Klan, who at that time were trying to negotiate with Elijah Muhammad so that they could make available to him a large area of land in Georgia or I think it was South Carolina. They had some very responsible persons in the government who were involved in it and who were willing to go along with it. They wanted to make this land available to him so that his program of separation would sound more feasible to Negroes and therefore lessen the pressure that the integrationists were putting upon the white man. I sat there. I negotiated it. I listened to their offer. And I was the one who went back to Chicago and told Elijah Muhammad what they had offered. Now, this was in December of 1960.

The code name that Jeremiah gave the Klan leader was 666. Whenever they would refer to him they would refer to him as Old Six. What his name was right now escapes me. But they even sat there and told stories how—what they had done on different escapades that they had been involved in. Jeremiah was there and his wife was there and I was there and the Klan was there.

From that day onward the Klan never interfered with the Black Muslim movement in the South. Jeremiah attended Klan rallies, as you read on the front page of the New York Tribune. They never bothered him, never touched him. He never touched a Muslim, and a Muslim never touched him. Elijah Muhammad would never let me go back down since January of 1961. I never went South, as long as I remained in the Black Muslim movement, again, from January of 1961, because most of the actions the Muslims got involved in was action that I was involved in myself. Wherever it happened in the country, where there was an action, it was action that I was involved in, because I believed in action. I never have gone along with no Ku Klux Klan.

And another one that he had made a deal with was this man Rockwell. Rockwell and Elijah Muhammad are regular correspondents with each other. You can hate me for telling you this, but I'm going to tell it to you. Rockwell attended the rally because Elijah Muhammad put the okay on it. And Sharrieff, the captain of the FOI, and I had discussed it, wondering why Rockwell could come to our meeting because it didn't help us. But Elijah Muhammad said let him in, so he had to be let in. No one questioned what Elijah Muhammad said. Now, if you doubt that this is true, you get all of the back issues of Muhammad Speaks newspaper and you will find articles in it about the Ku Klux Klan actually praising him. Jeremiah interviewed—I think it was—J.B. Stoner for the Muslim newspaper, and the old devil even gave him a contribution that he reported about in that paper. Sure he did.

When the brothers in Monroe, Louisiana, were involved in trouble with the police, if you'll recall, Elijah Muhammad got old Venable. Venable is the Ku Klux Klan lawyer. He's a Ku Klux Klan chieftain, according to the Saturday Evening Post, that was up on the witness stand. Go back and read the paper and you'll see that Venable was the one who represented the Black Muslim movement in Louisiana.

Now, brothers and sisters, until 1961, until 1960, until just before Elijah Muhammad went to the East, there was not a better organization among Black people in this country than the Muslim movement. It was militant. It made the whole struggle of the Black man in this country pick up momentum because of the unity, the militancy, created by the Muslim movement lent weight to the struggle of the Black man in this country against oppression.

But after 1960, after Elijah Muhammad went over there in December of '59 and came back in January of '60—when he came back, the whole trend or direction that he formerly had taken began to change. And in that change there's a whole lot of other things that had come into the picture. But he began to be more mercenary. More interested in money. More interested in wealth and, yes, more interested in girls.

And I guess many of you have heard it said that his financial support comes from a rich man in Texas. I heard that while I was in the movement. I've heard it more since I left the movement. A rich man in Texas. You can look up, any of you can look up his name. But the FBI knows that too. But they still don't touch him. And never have I seen a man—and this rich man who lives in Texas, by the way, lives in Dallas. His headquarters is in Dallas, his money is in Dallas, the same city where President John F. Kennedy was assassinated. And never have I seen a man in my life more afraid, more frightened than Elijah Muhammad was when John F. Kennedy was assassinated. I've never in my life seen a man as frightened as he was. And when I made the statement that I did, why he almost cracked up behind it because there were all kinds of implications to it that at that time were way above and beyond my understanding.

Now you may wonder, why is it so important to many interests for the Black Muslim movement to remain? But I told you, it has the most militant, most uncompromising, most dissatisfied Black people in America in it. Many have left it, many are still in it. The fear has been that if anything happened to Elijah Muhammad and the Black Muslim movement were to crumble, that all those militants who formerly were in it and were held in check would immediately become involved in the civil rights struggle, and they would add the same kinds of energy to the civil rights struggle that they gave to the Black Muslim movement. And there's a great fear. You know yourself, white people don't like for Black people to get involved in anything to do with civil rights unless those Black people are nonviolent, loving, patient, forgiving, and all of that. They don't like it otherwise.

And there has been a conspiracy across the country on the part of many factions of the press to suppress news that would open the eyes of the Muslims who are following Elijah Muhammad. They continue to make him look like he's a prophet somewhere who is getting some messages direct from God and is untouchable and things of that sort. I'm telling you the truth. But they do know that if something were to happen and all these brothers, their eyes were to come open, they would be right out here in every one of these civil rights organizations making these Uncle Tom Negro leaders stand up and fight like men instead of running around here nonviolently.

So they hope Elijah Muhammad remains as he is for a long time because they know that any organization that he heads, it will not do anything in the struggle that the Black man is confronted with in this country. Proof of which, look how violent they can get. They were violent, they've been violent from coast to coast. Muslims, in the Muslim movement, have been involved in cold, calculated violence. And not at one time have they been involved in any violence against the Ku Klux Klan. They're capable. They're qualified. They're equipped. They know how to do it. But they'll never do it—only to another brother. Now, I am well aware of what I'm setting in motion by what I'm saying up here tonight. I'm well aware. But I have never said or done anything in my life that I wasn't prepared to suffer the consequences for.

Marcus Garvey: Another Path

Wilson Jeremiah Moses

December 29, 2008

IIP Digital

There is a legend that once a Congolese leader in a remote African village was asked if he knew anything about the United States. His response was said to be, "I know the name of Marcus Garvey."

Under the name of the Black Star Line, the UNIA launched an abortive attempt to open up the world to black-owned commerce. The organization sold impressive amounts of stock in this enterprise, mostly in small amounts to ordinary working people, and purchased several steamships, unfortunately in dilapidated condition.

Garvey believed in separation of the races and was willing to cooperate with leaders of white racist organizations, notably the Ku Klux Klan. After meeting with Klan leadership, he came under attack from several already-hostile black leaders. A. Philip Randolph, founder and leader of the Brotherhood of Sleeping Car Porters, America's earliest successful, predominantly black labor union, was particularly hostile.

Randolph accused Garvey of cooperating with white racists in a scheme to repatriate American blacks back to Africa. Garvey denied any such ambitions, but he did send emissaries to the Republic of Liberia to investigate the prospects of new business undertakings, and he found considerable sympathy for his ideas among young African intellectuals.

In 1925, Garvey was imprisoned on federal charges of using the mails to defraud. He denied the charge, and even some of his critics found it unfair. President Calvin Coolidge pardoned Garvey in 1927, but as a convicted felon who was not a U.S. citizen, Garvey was immediately deported to his native Jamaica.

W.E.B. Du Bois, one of Garvey's severest critics, wished him well, encouraging him to pursue his efforts in his own country.

Establishing himself in London, England, Garvey launched a new magazine, The Black Man, which criticized such prominent black American figures as the heavyweight boxing champion Joe Louis, the entertainer and political activist Paul Robeson, and the controversial spiritual figure Father Divine for their failure to supply effective race leadership. But Garvey was unable there either to rebuild his organization to its previous membership levels. He retained sufficient U.S. popularity to draw an attentive audience to a meeting in Windsor, Ontario, just across the river from Detroit, Michigan, a base for Garvey's earlier activism. His final operations were conducted from London, England, where he died in 1940.

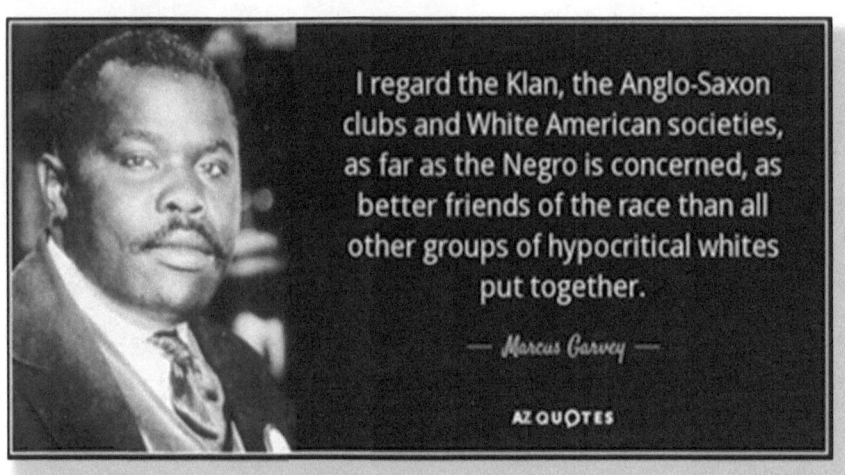

172.

Sister M. Tiggs El of Temple 9 said the Holy Prophet said, "You say that you want some pure meat to eat, no one is going to kill a camel for you to eat over here"

The Preservation of Camel Meat.
The Old Foodie.com
June 03, 2015

I have given you several 'curious' recipes from The Family receipt-book, or, Universal repository of useful knowledge and experience in all the various branches of domestic economy (London, 1810) and I have made another selection for you today. You may not have any camel flesh at hand, but as the recipe states, the method lends itself to other meats too. Of course it is entirely possible that trying this out might lead you to break several local food laws, but that is your risk!

Curious Moorish Method of preparing Elcholle, or the Flesh of Camels, as well as Mutton and Beef, so as to Keep for Two or Three Years in the warmest Climates. This favorite food of the Moors, which they call elcholle, whether made of beef, mutton, or camel's flesh, is always ready for eating; and will keep perfectly good two or three years, even in their hot climate. The method of preparing it is said to be as follows—Cut the meat, of whatever kind, but beef is the most esteemed, into long slices; and, having well salted them, let them remain twenty-four hours in the pickle. Then remove them into other vessels, filled with cold water; and, after thus soaking them all night, lay them on ropes, in the sun and air, till they become quite dry and hard. After this, cut them into pieces of about three inches long; throw them into a pot of warm oil, mixed with melted suet, sufficient to cover all the meat; and, when it has boiled till it looks clear and red on being cut, take the whole out, and set it to drain and cool. It is thus ready to put away in the jars provided for keeping it; and, on being there deposited, is covered with the oil and grease in which it was boiled. When quite cold, the jars are closely stopped; and the meat will thus be preserved hard, and continue good, for at least two or three years. In this state, it is often eaten by the Moors; who consider it, when hardest, as best and most palatable. They sometimes fry it with eggs and garlic; and, occasionally, eat it stewed, with a little lemon juice squeezed over it. European travelers, who have frequently tasted this elcholle of the Moors, pronounce it to be a very good dish, eaten either hot or cold.

178.

Sister M. Howell-Bey of Temple 19 said that the Holy Prophet said, "This food here is, just European poison."

The Dark Historical Roots of Our 'Thanksgiving' Lest We Forget...
Tristan Ahtone
Rence.com
November 26, 2003

The arrival of Europeans on the east coast of North America occurred not in 1620, but well before. French and Dutch fishermen and settlers had been in the area as early as 1614, and had been responsible for kidnapping Indians, selling them into slavery, and maliciously infecting them with smallpox.

In 1620, the pilgrims arrived on the east coast and within two days they had received assistance from the local Wampanoag Indian tribe: The pilgrims stole their stored crops, dug up graves for dishes and pots, and took many native people as prisoners and forced them to teach crop planting and survival techniques to the colonists in their new environment.

Luckily, for the colonists, an ex-slave named Squanto had recently escaped slavery in England, spoke English fluently and was able to instruct the pilgrims in crop planting, fishing, and hunting. Squanto not only escaped from slavery, he was also one of the only survivors of his tribe, and the rest had been wiped out from the European smallpox plagues years before. When it came to helping the rag-tag team of colonists, Squanto, not only was able to put aside his personal differences with the people who had enslaved him and killed off his entire tribe, but also helped make the colonists self-sufficient, and aided in brokering a treaty with the Wampanoag tribe. In 1621 Massasoit, the chief of the Wampanoag, signed a "treaty of friendship" giving the English permission to occupy 12,000 acres of land.

In 1621 the myth of thanksgiving was born. The colonists invited Massasoit, chief of the Wampanoag, to their first feast as a follow up to their recent land deal. Massasoit in turn invited 90 of his men, much to the chagrin of the colonists. Two years later the English invited a number of tribes to a feast "symbolizing eternal friendship." The English offered food and drink, and two hundred Indians dropped dead from unknown poison.

181.

Before the bank crash in 1929, Sister A. Brown El of Temple 4 and 25 said that the Holy Prophet told the Moors, "If they had money in the bank, to get it out". Some said that the Prophet told the Moors to put their money in the post office. Those that obeyed the Holy Prophet saved their money, and those that did not, lost their money. Bro. C. Carriton Bey (past) G.G. of New York said that one day he was at the annual national convention, and Bro. C. Kirkman Bey sent for him to come outside to witness something. There was a European man, his wife, and daughter there. The European man asked Bro. C. Kirkman-Bey "Where is that little man that use to be around." Bro. C. Kirkman-Bey let them know that he was no longer with us. These Europeans started crying. They were looking for the Holy Prophet. That man was able to save his money during the bank crash, because he obeyed the Holy Prophet, and took his money out of the bank.

Three weeks that changed the world
Nick Mathiason
The Guardian Online
December 27; 2008

It was the year the neo-liberal economic orthodoxy that ran the world for 30 years suffered a heart attack of epic proportions. Not since 1929 has the financial community witnessed 12 months like it. Lehman Brothers went bankrupt. Merrill Lynch, AIG, Freddie Mac, Fannie Mae, HBOS, Royal Bank of Scotland, Bradford & Bingley, Fortis, Hypo and Alliance & Leicester all came within a whisker of doing so and had to be rescued.

Western leaders, who for years boasted about the self-evident benefits of light-touch regulation, had to sink trillions of dollars to prevent the World Bank system collapsing.

The ramifications of the Banking Collapse of 2008 will be felt for years if not decades to come. Here, Observer writers pick out the three pivotal weeks that shaped a year of unforgettable and remarkable events.

Week one: 9-15 March

For the first two months of the year, there was an eerie calm. By the end of February, all was quiet save for global banks routinely updating queasy investors over the tens of billions of dollars they had lost by fueling the madness we now know as the debt catastrophe.

At the start of the year, a global economic meltdown still seemed unimaginable to many. Even Rupert Murdoch's economic brain Irwin Stelzer refused to countenance that the financial world was spinning off its axis, suspending judgment until a $150bn tax rebate by George Bush announced in January - equivalent to $1,000 for every American household - worked its way through the system. If by May that didn't stem a freefall in US consumer confidence, rising unemployment and plunging house prices, then he argued, perhaps we were in trouble.

But, during the first two months of the year, a lingering belief remained that perhaps the vicious economic hurricane might blow itself out before it hit the real world. That changed during the week beginning 9 March, seven days in which the real storm broke and swept away some of the biggest and most revered names in international finance.

It began on Sunday evening with an unbelievable personal fall from grace and ended with the most spectacular American banking collapse seen in decades.

Late that night, Eliot Spitzer, New York governor and the scourge of Wall Street banks, called his closest aides. The former New York attorney-general, who did more than anyone to prosecute bulge-bracket banks following the scandalous fin de siècle ramping up of internet stocks, admitted he had been caught on a wiretap confirming plans to a young woman to join him in a private room at the so-called Emperors' Club where New York's wealthy elite bed prostitutes.

As the once proud defender of the people against the excesses of capitalism sank into the quicksand, financial storm clouds swiftly gathered overhead.

The following day, Blackstone Group, manager of the world's biggest buyout fund, revealed it had suffered a 90 per cent profit drop during its fourth quarter.

185.

The Holy Prophet said, "I am going to make the European enforce my law."

Proclamations Affirming Moors Are Aboriginals

Many active and conscious Moorish-Americans across our North continent (America) have been consistent and dedicated in their duties and responsibilities to answer up to their constitution principles. In exercising their (our) Unalienable Rights and their (our) Divine Birthrights, Moors have been working to take their places in the affairs of men.

On December 22, 2011, Rahm Emanuel, Mayor of Chicago (Mecca) published a Proclamation that affirmed that Moors are the aboriginal and indigenous people of North America, South America, Central America and the adjoining Islands. To date "7" other City Officials have proclaimed the very same proclamation.

A Proclamation is the act of 'Proclaiming' or 'Publishing', which is an 'Avowel' (open Declaration) or a formal 'Decleration'. This act causes some 'State' matters to be 'Published' or to be made generally known; and by virtue of the said 'matter' being placed in 'written form' and issued by proper authority.

United States North American Republic Constitution, Article IV, Section 1

Article IV

Section 1. Full faith and credit shall be given in each state to the public acts, records, and judicial proceedings of every other state. And the Congress may by general laws prescribe the manner in which such acts, records, and proceedings shall be proved, and the effect thereof.

Location / Territory:	Public Servant Office / Official:	Day:
Chicago, Illinois	Rahm Emanuel, Mayor	December 22, 2011
Omaha, Nebraska	Jim Smith, Mayor	January 5, 2012
Tacoma, Washington	Marilyn Strickland, Mayor	January 4, 2012
Charlotte, North Carolina	Anthony R. Foxx, Mayor	January, 2012
Baltimore, Maryland	Stephanie Rawlings, Mayor	January 8, 2012
Fayetteville, North Carolina	Anthony G. Chavonne	January, 2012
Lynchburg, Virginia	Joan F. Foster, Mayor	January 2012
Little Rock, Arkansas	Mark Stodola, Mayor	January 8, 2012
Trenton, New Jersey	Tony Mack, Mayor	January, 2012
Tyler, Texas	Barbara Bas, Mayor	January, 2012
Atlanta, Georgia	C.T. Martin, Council Member	January 2012
Previous Proclamations / Resolutions:		
Washington, D.C.	Mayor, "Noble Drew Ali Day"	September 2011
Philadelphia, Pennsylvania	John Street, Mayor "Noble Drew Ali Day"	January, 2001
Philadelphia, Pennsylvania	David Cohen, Pres. City Council	September, 1991
Philadelphia, Pennsylvania	Senate Resolution #75 "Use of 'names' - Boys and Els"	April, 1933
Sundry Free Moore South Carolina	State Records of South Carolina Journal of The House of Representatives	January 1790

Compliments of R.V. Bey Publications - Revised January 2013

186.

Bro. T. Booker-Bey, Grand Natl. Treasurer (Emeritus) said that the Holy Prophet said, "The Moors were living up and down the Mississippi river before the European man came here" (that is the Moors were living up and down the Mississippi river before the Europeans came to the United States of America).

Uncovering America's Pyramid Builders
The Grandest Culture North of the Maya Created a City of 20,000 People, Built Monuments Rivaling Egypt's Great Pyramid, Then Vanished Into Oblivion
Karen Wright, Grant Delin
Discover Magazine
February 05, 2004

When U.S. 40 reaches Collinsville, Illinois, the land is flat and open. Seedy storefronts line the highway: a pawnshop, a discount carpet warehouse, a taco joint, a bar. Only the Indian Mound Motel gives any hint that the road bisects something more than underdeveloped farmland.

This is the Cahokia Mounds State Historic Site, a United Nations World Heritage Site on a par with the Great Wall of China, the Egyptian pyramids, and the Taj Mahal. The 4,000-acre complex preserves the remnants of the largest prehistoric settlement north of Mexico, a walled city that flourished on the floodplain of the Mississippi River 10 centuries ago. Covering an area more than five miles square, Cahokia dwarfs the ancient pueblos of New Mexico's Chaco Canyon and every other ruin left by the storied Anasazi of the American Southwest. Yet despite its size and importance, archaeologists still don't understand how this vast, lost culture began, how it ended, and what went on in between.

A thousand years ago, no one could have missed Cahokia—a complex, sophisticated society with an urban center, satellite villages, and as many as 50,000 people in all. Thatched-roof houses lined the central plazas. Merchants swapped copper, mica, and seashells from as far away as the Great Lakes and the Gulf of Mexico. Thousands of cooking fires burned night and day. And between A.D. 1000 and 1300, Cahokians built more than 120 earthen mounds as landmarks, tombs, and ceremonial platforms.

The largest of these monuments, now called Monks Mound, still dominates the site. It is a flat-topped pyramid of dirt that covers more than 14 acres and once supported a 5,000-square-foot temple. Monks Mound is bigger than any of the three great pyramids at Giza outside Cairo. "This is the third or fourth biggest pyramid in the world, in terms of volume," says archaeologist Tim Pauketat of the University of Illinois at Urbana-Champaign. It towers **100** feet over a 40-acre plaza that was surrounded by lesser mounds and a two-mile-long stockade. The monument was the crowning achievement of a mound-building culture that began thousands of years earlier and was never duplicated on this continent.

Islamic Leader in Trinidad and Tobago (1800's)

208.

The Holy Prophet Noble Drew Ali said "The garment that I have on represents power and if you obey my voice, you will have power with me." The Holy Prophet said "I am going to free you, though it's hard, because of your mixture, which brings about many different spirits." The Holy Prophet said "When you fail to hear my voice, you are lost." The Holy Prophet said "It is against the law to stand up in any audience intoxicated. The leader is not to stay out all night, giving earnings away to someone else. You who are heads of Temples, it is easy for you to destroy the influence of the Temple; now lace up your shoes, and get right." The Holy Prophet said "You, stop figuring out your way, how your salvation shall come, just follow me. You can say one thing Moors, you have made a start for the kingdom. If you want success, you must follow the Prophet." The Holy prophet said "Husbands take care of your wives, and families. Wives keep your homes and children clean." The Holy Prophet said "I have done more than you think. I want you to help me by your good deeds of living at home, and abroad. It is through your good, not with your lips, trying to be the front seat in everything, always standing in my face." The Holy prophet said "Moors, be careful of your steps, leaders of Temples must be careful how they walk. They must be an example." The

Holy Prophet said "I am not asleep, it will take you Moors a long time to find out what I did today. When you all go home, don't start no stuff, for I will be right there listening at you." The Holy Prophet Noble Drew Ali also said, "This is no social organization, it is a divine and national movement. By you being born here doesn't make you a citizen" (one must proclaim his nationality to be recognized as a citizen). "Look what I have on, now this was handed to me by the government. It represents the royal prince." (The Holy Prophet wore a mantle of power. There is a chapter in the Holy Koran of Mecca titled "He is mantled"). Sister M. Whitehead El (who is Sister M. Lovett El, (Past) G.G. of Illinois, and who was the Holy Prophet's wife's aunt. She was the aunt of Sister Pearl Ali. Said the Holy Prophet said in 1925 that, "I have mended the broken wires, and have connected them with the higher powers."

236.

The Holy Prophet said, "I am the fifth, and last Prophet, and I am five times more powerful than I was before." (The Prophet Noble Drew Ali was the last five Prophets that Allah sent, and He is five times more powerful than the others five Prophets before Him).

242.

Sis. Whitehead El stated that the Holy Prophet said "You stop figuring out your way how your salvation shall come, just follow me. You can say one thing Moors, you have made a start for the kingdom. If you want success you must follow the Prophet. Husbands, take care of your wives and families. Wives keep your homes and children clean. I have done more than you think. I want you all to help me by your good deeds of living at home and abroad. It is through your good not with lips, trying to be the front seat in everything always standing in my face. Moors be careful of your steps, leaders of Temples must be careful how they walk. They must be an example. I am not asleep, it will take you Moors a long time to find out what I did today. When you all go home don't start no stuff, for I will be right there listening at you."

248.
Bro. J. Blakely Bey stated that the Holy Prophet said "don't think that a fez or a turban on your head makes you a Moslem, Moslems are born, not made."

251.
Bro. J. Blakely Bey stated that the Holy Prophet said "many of you who think you are running away from the Prophet don't know that the further you run away from me, the closer you are coming to me, and when you wind up running you will be right in my arms."

254.
Bro. J. Blakely Bey stated that the Holy Prophet said "these Verbal Laws are Everlasting and Eternal just as much as my Written Laws."

258.
The Prophet said "Hold me up and I will draw all men unto you."

Other Predictions from the Prophet Noble Drew Ali

"If you doubt that I am a Prophet, watch my Prophesies"
Prophet Drew Ali

1. The Holy Prophet Noble Drew Ali told the Moors, "*I brought you everything it takes to save a nation, take it and save yourself.*" When He said that, the Prophet was holding up a Holy Koran of the Moorish Science Temple of America and a Questionnaire to show us the books we need to save ourselves.

2. The Holy Prophet told the Moors, "*Children, you are at home, and the European is 3,000 miles from home, and he is going to have to take some water*". Reported by Bro. O. Payton Bey, Temple #25, Detroit, Michigan.

3. Bro. I. Cook Bey and other Moors said The Holy Prophet said, "*My good Moors are going to live.*"

4. The Holy Prophet said, "*I am going to stop the European from thinking, and start you [Moors] to thinking for your own good.*"

5. Sister A. Brown El of Temple #25 said that the Holy Prophet said, "*If you got people in the South, get them out, because that is where destruction is going to start.*"

6. The Holy Prophet told The Moors, "*For the various lynchings and murders that were committed in the South; the South is going to have to pay off, and pay off in blood.*"

7. Bro. J. Foster Bey of Temple #4 and #25 said the Holy Prophet would say, "*Every word that I speak is spirit, and you Moors had better heed.*"

8. See page 8.

9. Bro. J. Foster Bey, Asst. Grand Sheik of Temple #25 and a member of Temple #4 in the 1920's said that the Holy Prophet said, "*When the fire comes, I will be the water.*"

10. Moors that saw and heard the Holy Prophet said that He said, "*What are all these people doing here. There is only going to be a handful saved. I can count them on my fingers, and have fingers left over.*"

11. Sister M. Payton Bey of Temple 4 and 25 said that the Holy Prophet

Noble Drew Ali said, "*I have got airplanes, zeppelins, and apparatus. I am going to take my good Moors up in an apparatus on an incline until it's all over with.*"

12. Bro. B. Jones El of Temple #43 heard the Holy Prophet, say, "*One day, they are going to tear down all the churches and take the bells and melt them down, and make bullets to fight with.*"

13. Bro. J. Blakely Bey said that the Holy Prophet Noble Drew Ali said, "*One day, every wheel of industry is going to stop, and when they start up again, it will be in the Asiatics' favor.*"

14. See page 11.

15. Bro. J. Blakely Bey said that the Holy Prophet Noble Drew Ali said, "*In the year 2000, the Moors will come into their own.*"

16. Bro. O. Payton Bey of Temple #4 and #25 said that the Holy Prophet said, "*One day your biggest trouble won't be getting with European women, it will be fighting them off.*"

17. See page 13.

18. Sister M. Tiggs El said that the Holy Prophet told the Moors that "*Before the European came here (to North America), that the bananas were large, and the grapes were four in hand, it took two men with hand sticks to carry one bunch of grapes.*"

19. The Holy Prophet told the Moors that "*When destruction comes, I am going to leave enough fine buildings, so that my good Moors will be able to enjoy them.*"

20. Bro. G. Cook Bey, Grand Sheik of Temple #1 said that the Holy Prophet said, "*One day, women are going to be chasing men like a hound running after a rabbit.*"

21. Bro. T. Booker Bey, Grand National Treasurer said that the Holy Prophet said, "*The European will not be able to remove all the wealth from the land. After he goes back to Europe, mountains of gold would be revealed to the Moors.*"

22. Bro. B. Jones El of Temple #43 heard the Holy Prophet say, "*Children, you are just plain rich.*"

23. Bro. J. Blakely Bey said that the Holy Prophet said, "*The European is going to have to pay our people off for the work that they did in slavery, and pay off in compounded interest.*"

24. See page 17.

25. Bro. I. Cook Bey, Grand Governor of Illinois, said that the Holy Prophet said. "*One day, the Europeans are going to lock the food*

up in warehouses, put soldiers around them to guard them, and you will go anywhere he says to get something to eat."

26. Sister A. Brown El of Temple #4 and #25 said that the Holy Prophet said, "*One day the European is going to let you down. You are going to have to put up a 90 day supply of food to last you until your brothers come to your rescue from the East.*"

27. Bro. R. Wise Bey of Temple #4 and #25 said that the Holy Prophet said, "*One day, some of you old Moors are going to be so hungry that you are going to bite into your own flesh, and blood will skeet out, and you are going to get angry with yourself, because you didn't put up enough food.*"

28. *See page 20.*

29. Bro. T. Booker Bey, Grand National Treasurer said that the Holy Prophet said, "*The Moors were once sea faring people and fed the world, the time is going to come, when we would go back and feed the world again*".

30. The Holy Prophet Noble Drew Ali showed Bro. T. Booker Bey and some other Moors one night, a spot in Chicago, Illinois, where a Moabite Queen ruled from. Her name was Queen Netha (Neith?), and she waged war against five Pharaohs. At that spot, the Holy Prophet dug down into the ground, and pulled up a metal bar with foreign writing on it.

31. *See page 24.*

32. *See page 27.*

33 *See page 30.*

34. The Holy Prophet told the Moors to "*Try to live close together.*"

35. Bro. J. Foster Bey of Temple #4 and #25 heard the Holy Prophet aid, "*We (The Moors) have the blood of every nation flowing through our veins, thereby bringing about a cross spirit.*"

36. Sister M. Payton Bey of Temple #4 and #25 heard the Holy Prophet say, "*The Italians have our blood (The blood of the Moors) mixed in their veins, that is why they are so mean.*"

37 *See page 34.*

38. Bro. I. Cook Bey, Grand Governor of Illinois heard the Holy Prophet speak a parable. He said, "*I remember when I was on the soul plane. I remember when I was Noah. Noah was a carpenter, and he built the Ark. When the flood came, men came swimming out to the Ark, and knocked on the door, and said,*

'Noah, Noah, let us in,' and I told them, 'The door is locked, and an angel came, and took the key away.'"

39. Bro. I. Cook Bey. Grand Governor of Illinois told Bro. R. Love El, Grand Sheik of the M.S.T. of A. and Bro. C. Tyson Bey, Chairman of the M.S.T. of A. reported about the time, when the Holy Prophet Noble Drew Ali and Bro. C. Kirkman Bey went to the Pan American Conference in 1928. At that time, the Holy Prophet went there and represented the Moors, and there was an Indian Chief representing the American Indians. The Conference was in Havana, Cuba, and the nations of North, South and Central America were present. Former Secretary of State Hughes of the United States represented the United States at this conference. Bro. C. Kirkman Bey was the interpreter for the Holy Prophet at this conference. Bro. I. Cook Bey said that when the Holy Prophet and Bro. C. Kirkman Bey's ship was tied up at the dock, the Cuban army was standing on the dock, and Bro. Kirkman Bey said something to them in Spanish, and the army came to attention, then he and the Holy Prophet came down from the ship. At the conference, Bro. C. Kirkman Bey addressed the conference in both Spanish and Arabic, and when the former Secretary of State of the United States, Charles Evans Hugh heard Bro. Kirkman Bey speak, he said, "That's a dangerous man." Up to that period of time, the United States was operating off of an expired 50 year mandate for this land. At this conference, the mandate for this land was reportedly given to Prophet Noble Drew Ali. Bro. G. Cook Bey, Grand Sheik of Temple One reportedly said that "**Prophet Noble Drew Ali showed us the mandate in the Adept Chamber**."

40. See page 37.

41. Sister M. Lovett El, Grand Governor of Illinois said that the Holy Prophet Noble Drew Ali said, "*I had to go around my elbow to get to my thumb to get what I wanted established in this government.*"

42. Sister M. Howell Bey of Temple #19 said that the Holy Prophet Noble Drew Ali, while speaking would jump up in the air and laugh, and say "*Rome, 2000 years ago, you got me, but I got you today.*"

43. Sister M. Lovett Bey, Grand Governor of Illinois said that the Holy Prophet Noble Drew Ali said, "*I placed a ball on Babylon, and it is rolling down, and anyone that gets in the way, is going to be ground to powder.*"

44. Bro. I. Cook Bey, Grand Governor of Illinois and other Moors said that the Holy Prophet said, "*You tore up everything that was brought to you, but I brought you something that you can't tear up. It will tear you up.*"

45. Sister A. Brown El of Temple #4 and #25 said that the Holy Prophet Noble Drew Ali said, "*I am going to leave the European here, just long enough to teach you how to run a government.*"

46. Sister M. Tiggs El of Temple #9 said that the Holy Prophet said, "*I am going to repeat myself.*"

47. Bro. G. Cook Bey, Grand Sheik of Temple #1 said that the Holy Prophet said that "*If you have a dream and you forget what you dreamed, to remember it, place your forehead face down on your pillow, and you will remember it.*"

48. The Holy Prophet said, "*If you dream of me, it is like seeing me for true, because the devil cannot steal my appearance.*"

49. Bro. T. Booker Bey, Grand Natl. Treasurer said that when at a meeting where the Holy Prophet was present, he saw ten Arabians, five Turks, two Chinese, and one Japanese join the Moorish Science Temple of America, and the Secretary asked the Holy Prophet Noble Drew Ali, "Prophet, these people have got their nationality, what should I put on their Nationality Card?" The Prophet said "*The Moors were the first people, and all other people that use our name were adopted in to our tribe.*"

50. See page 37.

51. Bro. J. Foster Bey of Temple #4 and #25 heard the Holy Prophet say, "*When the wild beast roamed the earth in large numbers, and you could hear the large birds flapping their wings at a long distance, it was the Moors that took the sword and went out and slayed the beast so that civilization could come in.*"

52. Sister M. Payton Bey of temple #4 and #25, and Bro. J. Davis Grand Governor of Michigan heard the Holy Prophet ask the Moors in Detroit, Michigan, "*How would you like to have your own Mayor and Chief of Police?*"

53. See page 40.

54. In the late 1920's, when there were thousands of Moors in the Moorish Science Temple of America, the Holy Prophet told the moors "*The membership is going to dwindle down to a handful, but keep the doors open, and I will drive the Asiatics in.*" The Holy Prophet said, "*When I drive the Asiatics in, it's going to take 10 secretaries, just to write the names down.*"

55. Bro. J. Blakely Bey said the Holy Prophet said, "*When I raise my flood gate, it's going to take 16 secretaries to write down the names.*"

56. Bro. O. Payton Bey Grand Sheik of Branch Temple #25 (Ecorse, Michigan) said that the Holy Prophet said, "*Let all old business stay as it is, and all new business, do it in your free national name.*"

57. See page 39.

58. Bro. J. Blakely Bey told the Moors that the Holy Prophet said that "*Things are going back to horse and buggy days.*"

59. Bro. B. Jones El, Assistant Grand Sheik of Temple #43 heard the Holy Prophet said, "*Children, one day, you are going to love me.*"

60. The Holy Prophet told the Moors, "*I am due in the East right now. I am going to have to go and straighten out the East, and then I will end up in the West. This (The West) will be the easiest. You will be able to be down and sleep, and wake up in peace. This will be, just a breakfast fight. By the time you eat breakfast, it will all be over with.*"

61. Bro. T. Booker Bey, Grand National Treasurer said the Holy Prophet said, "*One day, blood is going to flow in the streets up to a horse's brow.*"

62. See page 48.

63. The Holy Prophet asked the Moors, "*How many of you can do something?*" (Some say that he was inquiring as to how many of them could work magic, etc.) Some of the Moors stood up. The Prophet pointed his finger at them, and said, "*I am going to kill you all.*"

64. The Holy Prophet Noble Drew Ali said, "*Don't worry about how you are going to be saved. It will be done in a conflict that cannot be told in words.*"

65. Sister M. Payton Bey of Temple #4 and #25 said that the Holy Prophet said, "*I got here, just in time.*" She said that the Europeans were looking for him with airplanes, and with dreadnoughts. When the Holy Prophet came into the country (The U.S.) He was asked, "Where are those books that you have?" She said that the Prophet just smiled, but He told the Moors that He had the book in His head. When the Holy Prophet dictated verses of the Holy Koran of the Moorish Science Temple of America to the printer, He did it from memory. The printer was amazed!

66. Sister M. Payton Bey of Temple #4 and #25 said that the Holy Prophet said, "*I have got the world in a jug, and the stopper in my hand.*" Others said that the Holy Prophet said, "*I have got the world in a jug, and the stopper in my hand. I have got the Asiatic, and I have got the European. I have got the silver and*

I have got the gold."

67. Bro. J. Blakely Bey said that the Holy Prophet said, "*It will take 50 years to find out what I brought you, and if you are not careful, 50 years after I am gone, you won't know that I have been here.*"

68. The Holy Prophet told the Moors, "*I brought you something that you can shout about.*"

69. Bro. G. Cook Bey, Grand Sheik of Temple #1 related that he set up a meeting of Christian preachers to meet with the Holy Prophet Noble Drew Ali to see whether these preachers would follow the Holy Prophet. Bro. G. Cook Bey had these ministers assembled, and he was addressing them before the Holy Prophet came to the meeting. One of the preachers said, "If He (speaking of the Holy Prophet) could do what Moses could, I would follow Him." The Holy Prophet was not present in the room when this statement was made, and the meeting place was on the third floor of the building that they were in. When the Holy Prophet arrived at the meeting, He told the preacher, "*I can do what Moses did, but if I came walking into the meeting with a lion on a chain, you would jump out of the window and kill yourself.*"

70. The Holy Prophet told the Moors "*Don't endanger your life with a fool.*"

71. Bro. J. Foster Bey of Temple #4 and #25 said that the Holy Prophet said, "*Before one jot or title of my word fail to come to pass, heaven and earth will pass away.*"

72. See page 51.

73. See page 53.

74. The Holy Prophet said, "*If my Principles are carried out (The Principles of Love, Truth, Peace, Freedom and Justice for our people in this land), the United States will be the richest and most prosperous country on the earth, if not, the worst is yet to come.*"

75. The Holy Prophet told the Moors, "*The times that have been, won't be no more.*"

76. The Holy Prophet let the Moors know that He was Jesus. He said, "*Those that were with me 2000 years ago, are with me today, and those that were against me 2000 years ago, are against me today.*"

77. Prophet Noble Drew Ali told the Moors, "*Moors, be yourself.*"

78. The Holy Prophet said, "*Moors, study yourself.*"

79. Sister Gaddy Bey of Tempe #4 and #25 said that the Holy Prophet said, "*Children, your hair is not kinky. It is woolly like your Brother Jesus.*"

80. Bro. T. Booker Bey. Grand National Treasurer said that the Holy Prophet said that "*The Moors were the off springs of Kings and Queens.*"

81. The Holy Prophet Noble Drew Ali said, "*Allah alone is perfect.*"

82. The Holy Prophet Noble Drew Ali said, "*Allah alone guides the destiny of the Moorish Science Temple of America.*"

83. Sister M. Howell Bey of Temple #19 said that the Holy Prophet said that when the Europeans asked him, "Will we be saved this time?" The Holy Prophet said, "*If you do, it will be through the Moors.*"

84. The Holy Prophet told the Moors that "*The Europeans were not going to give up until he looked death in the face.*"

85. Bro. J. Blakely Bey told the Moors that the Holy Prophet said, "*It doesn't make any difference which way things look like they are going, it's all going to end up in the Asiatics hands.*"

86. The Holy Prophet Noble Drew Ali told the Moors, "*Children, when you get on top, treat the European nice.*"

87. Sister M. Payton Bey of Temple #4 and #25 said that the Holy Prophet said, "*Let your good deeds out number your bad deeds, and when you pass away, you won't have anything to worry about.*"

88. Sister M. Payton Bey said that the Holy Prophet told the Moors, "*I have got spies everywhere.*"

89. Bro. J. Blakely Bey said that the Holy Prophet told the Moors, "*Not throw away your slave names (your family last name), because we have a birth right under them. For the work that our ancestors did in slavery time, we will be paid off for this, and with compounded interest.*"

90. The Holy Prophet told the Moors to "*Get a good European education, and I can use you.*"

91. *See page 56.*

92. Bro. O. Payton Bey of temple #4 and #25 said that the Holy Prophet said, "*Moors should learn Spanish as a second language.*"

93. Bro. W. Davis El, Grand Governor of Michigan said that the Holy Prophet said, "*Don't even carry a pocket knife.*"

94. Bro. J. Brown El of Temple #25 said that the Holy Prophet said, "*One

day, people are going to be so hungry that the only way that you will be able to turn them away, will be at the point of a gun."

95. Bro. J. Blakely Bey said that the Holy Prophet said, "*The third and fourth generation will see the good of my work.*"

96. Sister A. Brown El of Temple #4 and #25 said that the Holy Prophet told the Moors, "*Take a good look at me, so that you will know me when you see me.*" She also said that the Holy Prophet said, "*When you see me don't speak to me unless I speak to you first.*"

97. Bro. Smith Bey of Temple #3 and #9 stated that some Asiatics paid some hit men to kill the Holy Prophet. When the hit men went to the temple where the Holy Prophet was teaching, that they opened the door, and found the temple building full of soldiers. The hit men went back to the people that hired them, and told them, "Don't you pay us to do anything to any of those Moorish Americans."

98. *See page 59.*

99. *See page 60.*

100. Bro. J. Foster Bey of Temple #4 and #25 told the Moors that the Holy Prophet said. "*When the Moors ruled Spain, we had street lights in Seville, Spain 400 years before they had them anywhere else in Europe.*"

101. Bro. T. Booker Bey. Grand National Treasurer said that he was walking down the street in Chicago, Illinois, and an Arabian came out of a store, and asked him to come into the store. He went with him. The Arabian pointed at a man, and asked him. "Do you know who this is?" Bro. Booker Bey said, "That is my Prophet." The Holy Prophet said, "*All right son.*" The store was full of Arabians, and Bro. T. Booker Bey said that all of them had Nationality Cards for the Moorish Science Temple of America.

102. *See page 61.*

103. *See page 62.*

104. Sister E. Sims El of Temple #4 and #43 said that she went to the Holy Prophet, because she had been sick. The Holy Prophet listened to her, and said, "*Sister, you are going to get well.*" But that is as much of that meeting that she related, but her husband, Bro. R. Sims El, Grand Sheik of Temple #4 said that the Holy Prophet said to her also, "*Sister, go to the Temple, if you have got to crawl.*"

105. Sister A. Brown El of Temple #4 and #25 said that the Holy Prophet said in the 1920S, "*Some of my best Moors are still in the*

church."

106. Bro. O. Payton Bey of Temple #4 and #25 said that the Holy Prophet said, "*There are going to be new Moors that are going to come in with their eyes wide open, seeing and knowing, that are going to take you old Moors, seat you in the back, and carry out my law.*"

107. See page 63.

108. Bro. J. Foster Bey of Temple #4 and #25 told the Moors that the Holy Prophet said, "*I can throw out a spirit that would make the Moors want to fight, and then throw out another spirit that would bring them back to peace.*"

109. Bro. T. Booker Bey, Grand National Treasurer said at one night's temple meeting, a dirty Moor tried to attack the Holy Prophet with a knife. The Moors in attendance just stood there. After the event, the Holy Prophet told the Moors, "*I have got a good mind to leave you.*" Bro. T. Booker Bey said that the Moors got down on their knees, and begged the Prophet not to leave them. After their begging the Holy Prophet not to leave, a man appeared in the room that looked like a Turk, and he said, "If you harm a hair of his head (speaking of the Holy Prophet) we will come and destroy you all."

110. Sister A. Brown El of Temple #4 and #25 said that the Holy Prophet told the Moors that "*The climate was going to change. The cold weather will be in the South, and the warm weather will be in the North.*"

111. Bro. T. Booker Bey, Grand National Treasurer Grand National Treasurer said that the Holy Prophet said, "*I like good peas and beans. I am going to save 8% of the Europeans, because they are good farmers.*"

112. Sister A. Brown and Bro. C. Barker Bey said that the Holy Prophet told the Moors, "*Don't let none of those foreign Moslems get up in your rostrum.*"

113. Sister M. Tiggs El of Temple #9 said that the Holy Prophet said, "*One day, you are going to smell the Europeans before you see them, in boxcars, going back to Europe.*"

114. The Holy Prophet said. "*If you steal my money, it's going to burn up in your pocket.*"

115. Bro. J. Gill Bey of Temple #4 and #25 and the Moorish Home Office #1 said the Holy Prophet said. "*If you have money, and don't give it to me (to help out in the divine and national movement of*

the M.S.T. of A.), I am going to get it anyway."

116. The Holy Prophet told the Moors that "*One day, there are going to be so few people, that when you see an old Moor, you will run up to him, and kiss him all on top of his head.*"

117. The Holy Prophet told the Moors that "*There will be so few men, that a child will go to the store, and return home, and tell his mother, 'Mother, I saw a man.'*"

118. Sister M. Howell El of Temple #19 said that the Holy Prophet pointed his finger, and said, "*My sheep know the sound of my voice; a stranger will not follow.*"

119. Sister M. Howell El of Temple #19 said that the Holy Prophet told the Moors, "*I brought you your nationality, your religion, and title to your vast estate. What do you want me to do; kill you?*"

120. Bro. G. Cook Bey, Grand Sheik of Temple 1 said the Holy Prophet said, "*While I am talking to you Moors, my spirit is over in India with them, and those old sisters are jumping this high (They were jumping as high as He was holding his hand), because of my coming to them.*"

121. Sister M. Howell El said that the Holy Prophet told the Moors, "*I am going to burn up sin, both root and branch.*"

122. Sister M. Howell El said that Bro. C. Kirkman Bey told her that the Holy Prophet said, "*Anytime a Moslem goes into a church for any reason; it ceases to be church, and it is a temple.*"

123. Sister M. Howell El said that the Holy Prophet said, "*You can walk down the street by yourself now, but one day, you won't be able to do that.*"

124. Bro. I. Cook Bey, Grand Governor of Illinois said that the Holy Prophet said, "*I have got two wives. One day, you will be able to have two, or as many as you can afford.*"

125. Bro. O. Payton Bey of Temple #4 and #25 said that the Holy Prophet told the Moors, "*I am going to let the fire touch some of you old Moors' shirt tail.*"

126. Bro. T. Booker Bey, Grand National Treasurer said that the Holy Prophet told the Moors "*I am going to let the fire scorch some of my good Moors.*"

127. Bro. E. Thomas El of Temple #43 said the Holy Prophet said, "*Money will be burnt in the streets, and we won't be able to buy much; and when I put my spirit in the streets, you won't be able to sell your car for 25 cents.*"

128. Bro. E. Thomas said that the Holy Prophet said, "*The European will seek peace, but none shall be found.*"

129. Bro. E. Thomas El said that the Holy Prophet said, "*All nations will turn against the United States, one day.*"

130. See page 64.

131. Sister M. Howell Bey of Temple #19 said that the Holy Prophet said, "*I am going to stop the Europeans from thinking if two or three of them get together on something, they will go back, and tear it up.*"

132. During the time of the Holy Prophet, one of the Sisters in Chicago, Illinois was living loosely, and going in the alley to so act with her turban on. The Holy Prophet told the Moors, "*Stay out of the alley with your turbans on.*"

133. Bro. J. Foster Bey of Temple #4 and #25 told the Moors that the Holy Prophet told the Moors in Detroit, Michigan to "*Carry your fez to the temple.*" This was supposedly said because some Moors were wearing their fezzes in bars and other places of ill repute.

134. Bro. J. Blakely Bey told the Moors that the Holy Prophet told the Moors, "*People are going to be dying like hogs with the cholera, and the doctors won't know what is wrong with them. The only thing that is going to save them is my remedies.*"

135. Sister M. Lovett El Grand Governor of Illinois said that the Holy Prophet said, "*My remedies will cure you of anything that you weren't born with.*"

136. Bro. J. Blakely Bey said that the Holy Prophet said that "*We are going to be taxed to death.*"

137. See page 67.

138. J. Blakely Bey told the Moors that the Holy Prophet said, "*If you are not careful, your own brothers will try to put you in slavery.*"

139. See page 70.

140. Sister A. Brown El of Temple #4 and #25 said that the Holy Prophet said, "*One day, some of you Moors are going to be walking around with skippers (maggots) falling out of you, praying to die, and won't be able to die.*"

141. See page 75.

142. Sister M Payton Bey of Temple #4 and #25 said that the Holy Prophet said, "*Try to have your temples in buildings, where the*

meetings are on the second floor."

143. Bro. O. Payton Bey of Temple #4 and #25 said that the Holy Prophet said, "*I took the cover off all the secret organizations.*"

144. The Holy Prophet said, "*Imitate I, The Prophet.*" And He said, "*Moorish Leaders, live a life of love, so that you will be loved as I the Prophet is loved.*"

145. Sister M. Tiggs El said that the Holy Prophet said that "*At the End of time, those that will be in the apparatus will be able to look down on earth, see people that you know, fleeing for their life.*"

146. The Holy Prophet told the Moors that "*They sleep too much*".

147. Bro. I. Cook Bey, Grand Governor of Illinois said that the Holy Prophet told the Moors, "*Children, sow good seeds.*"

148. Sister, M. Payton Bey, Grand National Treasurer said that the Holy Prophet said, "*You are from Missouri, I have got to show you.*"

149. Bro. T. Booker Bey, Grand National Treasurer said that the Holy Prophet told the Moors, "*In two weeks, I am going down South. When I get down there, the Ku Klux Klan is going to stop me. At first, it is going to look like they are against me. Then they are going to lead me where I am going.*"

150. See page 78.

151. The Holy Prophet told the Moors, "*You are going to be saved in a conflict that cannot be told in words.*"

152. Sister A. Brown El of Temple #4 and #25 said that the Holy Prophet said, "*Don't throw away your Bibles, because I am going to use them to condemn the government.*"

153. The Holy Prophet said, "*This is the uniting of Asia.*"

154. Bro. G. Cook Bey, Grand Sheik of Temple #1 said that he asked the Holy Prophet to tell him about a particular star in the heavens, and the Holy Prophet told him," *If you go and get 10 people, I will tell you about that star.*" Bro. Cook Bey said that he could not get anyone, and he returned to the Holy Prophet, and informed him of that. The Holy Prophet told him, "*I could tell you some things that would turn your brain to water.*"

155. Bro. I Cook Bey, Grand Governor of Illinois, said that the Holy Prophet said, "*You can lead a horse to water, but you can't make him drink. I am going to lead some of you Moors all the way up to salvation, and you are going to turn around and go the other way.*"

156. Bro. I. Cook Bey said that the Holy Prophet said, "*I am a General as well as a Prophet.*" "*I was Mohammed. Mohammed defeated the Roman Empire. When I conquered Rome, we went in with the sword. You could hear the swords swinging. I cut the head of Rome off; pulled down the flags; sent letters to the other European governments, and asked them was I right. They said, "Yes Mohammed, you are right. Just let us have a place to live."* The Holy Prophet said, "*I went into Rome with 72,000 men. When I ran out or men, I reached down, and picked up a hand full of sand, I threw it up in the air, and when it came down, there were soldiers seated on camels.*"

157. Bro. I. Cook Bey said that the Holy Prophet said, "The *only thing that would surprise me, is if a Moor would do right.*"

158. Bro. I. Cook Bey said that the Holy Prophet said, "*One day, you are going to look for the good Moors, and you won't be able to find them.*"

159. Sister A. Brown El of Temple #4 and #25 said the Holy Prophet said, "*Your Nationality Card is going to change on you in your pocket.*"

160. The Holy Prophet said, "I *am not going to wake up all the Asiatics at once, because they may tear up something.*"

161. The Holy Prophet said, "*If my own mother is not right, I am not going to let her get by.*"

162. The Holy Prophet said, "*Pray you don't have to make your flight in the winter time.*"

163. Bro. J. Foster Bey of Temple #4 and #25 said that the Holy Prophet said, "*If you put your hand to the gospel plow and turn loose, it would be better, if you never took hold.*"

164. The Holy Prophet said, "*Woe upon the one that scatters my flock.*"

165. The Holy Prophet said, "*Woe upon the man that calls himself a Jew.*"

166. The Holy Prophet said, "*One day you will see a $20.00 bill in the street, and would not bend over to pick it up.*"

167. Bro. G. Cook Bey, Grand Sheik of Temple #1 said that the Holy Prophet Noble Drew Ali said, "*One day, you are going to look out into the streets, and the streets are going to be filled with men with turbans and fezzes, and the highways are going to be blocked.*"

168. The Holy Prophet said, "*A good Moorish leader must study his Holy Koran and Divine Constitution and By laws.*"

169. Sister M. Tiggs El of Temple #9 said that the Holy Prophet said, "*Cats are evil spirits, and if you knew what a black cat was, you would not want one around.*"

170. Sister M. Tiggs El of Temple #9 said that the Holy Prophet said, "*Don't keep dogs in your house, because if you inhale one of its hairs, it could cut your throat.*"

171. Sister M. Tiggs El of Temple #9 said the Holy Prophet said, "*You say that you want some pure meat to eat, no one is going to kill a camel for you to eat over here.*"

172. *See page 85.*

173. The Holy Prophet told the Moors, "*When children start crying in a meeting, take them out of the meeting.*"

174. Bro. G. Cook Bey, Grand Sheik of Temple One said that the Holy Prophet Noble Drew Ali said, "*I am going to save you all, if I have got to kill you all.*"

175. Bro. I. Cook Bey, Grand Governor of Illinois said that the Holy Prophet Noble Drew Ali said, "*If I cannot teach you here, I will teach you on the soul plane.*"

176. Sister M. Howell Bey of Temple #19 said that the Holy Prophet said, "*This food here is just European poison.*"

177. Bro. I. Cook Bey, Grand Governor of Illinois said that the Holy Prophet said, "*When I was born, it turned black dark in the day time. The people put their hoes down, and came out of the fields.*"

178. *See page 87.*

179. Before the bank crash in 1929, Sister A. Brown El of Temple #4 and #25 said that the Holy Prophet told the Moors, "*If you have money in the bank, get it out.*" Some said that the Prophet told the Moors to put their money in the post office. Those that obeyed the Holy Prophet saved their money, and those that did not, lost their money. Bro. C. Carriton Bey Grand Governor of New York said that one day he was at the annual national convention, and Bro. C. Kirkman Bey sent for him to come outside to witness something. There was a European man, his wife, and daughter there. The European man asked Bro. C. Kirkman Bey "Where is that little man that used to be around." Bro. C. Kirkman Bey let them know that he was no longer with us. These Europeans started crying. They were looking for the

Holy Prophet. That man was able to save his money during the bank crash, because he obeyed the Holy Prophet, and took his money out of the bank.

180. The Holy Prophet told the Brothers to "*Use kind words toward your wife.*"

181. *See page 89.*

182. Sister M. Lovett El, Grand Governor of Illinois said that the Holy Prophet said, "*One day, men are going to be running so fast that their coat tails will be standing straight out. You will be able to shoot dice on their coat tails. They are going to be running to get into the Temple. The last ones to make it into the temple will be the preachers, and the Europeans are going to be beating them over the head, driving them in.*"

183. The Holy Prophet said, "*I am going to make the European enforce my law.*"

184. Bro. T. Booker Bey, Grand Natl. Treasurer said that the Holy Prophet said, "*The Moors were living up and down the Mississippi river before the European man came here.*"

185. *See page 92.*

186. *See page 94.*

187. Bro. O. Payton Bey of Temple #4 and #25 said that the Holy Prophet said, "*When you take care of Temple business go in numbers of two, three, five, and seven.*"

188. Sister M. Payton Bey of Temple #4 and #25 said the Holy Prophet said, "*Everyone needs to have a secret.*"

189. Bro. I. Foster Bey, Bro. W. Davis El, Grand Governor of Michigan, and Bro. J. Blakely Bey, who were all members of Temple 4 in Detroit, Michigan during the lifetime of the Holy Prophet, all said that at one meeting, when the Holy Prophet was in Detroit speaking in the Temple, an Asiatic got up while the Holy Prophet was speaking and said, "If that man is a prophet, I would be willing to give up my life." This angered some of the Moors that heard it. Bro. W. Davis El said that some of the Moors started moving up on this man with their hands in their pockets, and they were going to cut him to death, but the Holy Prophet held up his hand, and said, "*Children, did you hear that? It is too bad.*" After the Holy Prophet spoke those words, this Asiatic fell back into his seat, and slumped down. When the meeting was over, the Moors carried him out of the building, he was dead.

190. Sister A, Brown El of Temple #4 and #25 said that the Holy Prophet said, "*If your Brother does something wrong to you, don't call him a "nigger." Call him a dirty Moor.*"

191. Bro. Smith Bey of Temple #3 and #9 said that the Holy Prophet Noble Drew Ali said, "*Boys, why don't you be like I, your Prophet. I don't drink, and I don't smoke, but if you do, don't stop it all at once. If you do, you may hurt something.*"

192. Sister M. Payton Bey of Temple #4 and #25 said that the Holy Prophet said, "*Don't drink and come to the temple, and sit down next to people with liquor on your breath.*"

193. Sister M. Payton Bey said that the Holy Prophet said, "*If you just have to drink, go into your room.*"

194. Sister M. Payton Bey said that the Holy Prophet said, "*If it were not for that little piece of red flannel, we would not get into so much trouble.*"

195. Sister M. Payton Bey said that the Holy Prophet said, "*The only thing that hurts a duck is his bill.*"

196. Sister M, Lovett El, Grand Governor of Illinois said that the Holy Prophet said, "*If I were you, I would get ready before you are made to do so.*"

197. Bro. O. Payton Bey of Temple #4 and #25 said that the Holy Prophet said, "*One day, the United States will not be able to do any business, unless they do it through the Asiatic.*"

198. Bro. I. Cook Bey, Grand Governor said that the Holy Prophet said "*Children, if you want to come up to see me, you can.*"

199. The Holy Prophet Noble Drew All said, "I *come to set you free from that state of mental slavery that I found you in.*"

200. Bro. J. Blakely Bey said that the Holy Prophet said, "*Don't put the European on your brother.*"

201. Sister A. Brown El of Temple #4 and #25 said that the Holy Prophet Noble Drew Ali said, "*If you go to an Adept Meeting, don't tell anyone who does not go, what happened at the meeting.*" (

202. The Holy Prophet said, "*A Moorish leader is not to get up to speak under the influence of liquor, or any harmful motive that will seek to break up the families of men.*"

203. Bro. O. Payton Bey of Temple #4 and #25 said that the Holy Prophet Noble Drew Ali said, "*If you have a wife, and she does not belong to the Temple, instead of giving her one apple, give her two.*"

204. Bro. O. Payton Bey of Temple #4 and #25 said that the Holy Prophet said, "*If someone assaults you, flee from him. If you cannot flee from him, turn around, and drop the world on him.*"

205. Bro. J. Blakely Bey said that the Holy Prophet said, "If *you don't leave here right with me this time, you won't make it back here in human form.*"

206. At the first National Moorish Science Temple of America convention, the Holy Prophet Noble Drew Ali said "*The garment that I have on represents power and if you obey my voice, you will have power with me. I am going to free you, though it's hard, because of your mixture, which brings about many different spirits. When you fail to hear my voice, you are lost. It is against the law to stand up in any audience intoxicated. The leader is not to stay out all night, giving earnings away to someone else. You who are heads of Temples, it is easy for you to destroy the influence of the Temple; now lace up your shoes, and get right. You, stop figuring out your way, how your salvation shall come, just follow me. You can say one thing Moors, you have made a start for the kingdom. If you want success, you must follow the Prophet. Husbands take care of your wives, and families. Wives keep your homes and children clean. I have done more than you think. I want you to help me by your good deeds of living at home, and abroad. It is through your good, not with your lips, trying to be the front seat in everything, always standing in my face. Moors, be careful of your steps, leaders of Temples must be careful how they walk. They must be an example.*" The Holy Prophet said "*I am not asleep; it will take you Moors a long time to find out what I did today. When you all go home, don't start no stuff, for I will be right there listening at you.*" The Holy Prophet Noble Drew Ali also said, "*This is no social organization, it is a divine and national movement. By you being born here doesn't make you a citizen.*" "*Look what I have on, now this was handed to me by the government. It represents the royal prince.*"

207. Sister M. Whitehead El cited the Holy Prophet in 1928 as saying, "*I have mended the broken wires, and have connected them with the higher powers.*"

208. See page 97.

209. Sister A. Brown El of Temple #4 and #25 said that the Holy Prophet said, "*Some of you Moors are going to throw away your name, just for a morsel of bread.*"

210. Sister M. Washington El of Temple #43 said that the Holy Prophet

said. "*One day, there is going to be a holy war.*"

211. The Holy Prophet Noble Drew Ali said, "*There is but one Allah, one Prophet of the Temple, and one Moorish Science Temple of America.*"

212. The Holy Prophet told the Moors, "I *have come, and taken away all the excuses.*"

213. Bro. J. Gill Bey of Temple #4 and the colony in Prince George, VA., said that the Holy Prophet said, "*I forgive you of everything that you did before I came, you are responsible for your deeds now.*"

214. Sister M. Payton Bey of Temple #4 and #25 said that the Holy Prophet said, "*If I tell you that I am going to do a thing, I have done it already.*"

215. Sister M. Payton Bey said that the Holy Prophet said, "*I have fixed everything; I have stopped up every rat hole.*"

216. The Holy Prophet Noble Drew Ali, "*I have come for the children, and the unborn generations.*"

217. Bro. I. Cook Bey, Illinois of Illinois said that the Holy Prophet said, "*There is going to be famine in the land.*"

218. The Holy Prophet Noble Drew Ali said, "*Chicago is going to be your new Mecca.*"

219. Bro. G. Cook Bey, Grand Sheik of Temple 1 said that the Holy Prophet Noble Drew Ali said, "The *only one that works all the time, is a coolie.*"

220. Bro. J. Blakely Bey said that the Holy Prophet Noble Drew Ali said that "*The Grand Sheik of a Temple should go to the Temple, hang the Charter on the wall, say the Moorish American prayer, when it is time for the meeting to open, and if no one comes to the meeting after he sits and waits for one and half hours, then take the Charter down off the wall and go home.*"

221. Sister M. Payton Bey of Temple #4 and #25 said that the Holy Prophet said, "*Before the End of Time, I am going to lower down the evil spirits, and let them incarnate.*"

222. Bro. J. Blakely Bey said that the Holy Prophet said, "I *would like to save half of the people, but I am going to try to save a fourth of the people.*" "*There is just going to be a handful saved. I can count them on my fingers, and have fingers left over*".

223. The Holy Prophet said, "*One day, all of the property is going back to the government.*"

224. Sister A. Brown El of Temple #4 and #25 said that the Holy Prophet said, "*Boil your drinking water.*"

225. Bro. J. Foster Bey while the Assistant Grand Sheik of Temple 25 told the Moors that the Holy Prophet told the Moors after a meeting, and most of the people had gone home, "*Wake up you sleepy headed Moors. I am going to take you up above the sun, moon and stars, around the throne of the Mighty Allah.*" Bro. J. Foster Bey said that the Holy Prophet took them up above the blue ethers, around the throne of Allah. This happened in Detroit, Michigan in the late 1920's. Bro. J. Foster Bey concluded with the words, "Moors, your Prophet was a Prophet."

226. Bro. T. Booker Bey, Grand National Treasurer, said that the Holy Prophet Noble Drew Ali said, "*I have got the Romans in the palm of my hand.*"

227. Bro. T. Booker Bey, Grand National Treasurer said that the Holy Prophet said, "*The Moors are a dangerous people. I am not going to wake you all up at once; if I do, I won't be able to do anything with you myself.*"

228. Sister M. Lovett El, Grand Governess, said that the Holy Prophet said, "*One day, there are going to be so many women, a man is going to have to run for his life.*"

229. Bro. T. Booker Bey, Grand National Treasurer said that the Holy Prophet Noble Drew Ali said, "*The Moors once ruled the world; now get ready to rule it again. But this time it's going to be done under Love, Truth, Peace, Freedom and Justice.*"

230. Bro. I. Cook Bey, Grand Governor of Illinois said that the Holy Prophet said, "*I can do what Jesus did, but you are not in the condition that those people were in.*"

231. Bro. J. Foster Bey of Temple #4 and #25 said that the Holy Prophet said, "*The European is our fellow man.*"

232. The Prophet said, "*Money does not make the man, and clothes do not make the man. It is character and free national standards that make the man.*"

233. Bro. O. Payton Bey, Grand Sheik of Branch Temple #25 (Ecorse, M.I.) said that the Holy Prophet said, "*If you try to tell what a man is by looking at him, you are burnt up from the start.*"

234. Bro. J. Foster Bey of Temple #4 and #25 said that the Holy Prophet said, "*If your brother wants something, give it to him so that he won't sin.*"

235. The Holy Prophet said, "*I am the fifth, and last Prophet, and I am five times more powerful than I was before.*"

236. See page 99.

237. During the First Annual National Convention in 1928, one of the Grand Governors of a State failed to appear at the Convention. Bro. J. Blakely Bey said that the Holy Prophet sent the Grand Governor a telegram informing him, that if he did not attend the Convention, that He (The Holy Prophet) was going to have the federal agents to arrest him.

238. The Holy Prophet told the Moors, "*When you get married, go before you Grand Sheik, and let him perform the ceremony*". Some of the Moors did not obey The Holy Prophet's order, so He told the Moors, "*Go downtown, and buy your wives from the Europeans.*"

239. Sis. Whitehead El stated that the Holy Prophet said "*The garment I have on represents power and if you obey my voice you will have power with me. I am going to free you though it's hard because of your mixture which brings about many different spirits. When you fail to hear my voice you are lost. It is against the law to stand up in any audience intoxicated. The leader is not to stay out all night diving earnings away to someone else. You, who are heads of Temples, it is easy for you to destroy the influence of the Temple and me. Now lace up your shoes and get right!*" Sis. Whitehead El stated that the Holy Prophet said "*Our nationality in this government began with the parade.*" Sis. Whitehead El stated the Holy Prophet said "*This is not no social organization it is a Divine and National Movement. By you being born here don't make you a citizen. Look what I have on, now this was handed to me by the government. It represents the Royal Prince.*"

240. Bro. J. Blakely Bey stated that the Holy Prophet said "*Above all Moors, don't put the European on your brothers.*"

241. Bro. J. Blakely Bey stated that the Holy Prophet said "*Don't try to deal out justice, for justice belongs to Allah, and Allah alone.*"

242. See page 100..

243. Bro. J. Blakely Bey stated that the Holy Prophet said "*Moors don't worry about the south, for I will take care of the south.*

244. Bro. J. Blakely Bey stated that the Holy Prophet said "*Don't think that a fez or a turban on your head makes you a Moslem, Moslems are born, not made.*"

245. Bro. J. Blakely Bey stated that the Holy Prophet said "*Islam can draw you or it can drive you, and Islam can save you or it can destroy you.*"

246. Bro. J. Blakely Bey stated that the Holy Prophet said "*I am going to drive the Moors back home to Islam if I have to cut their bread off.*"

247. Bro. J. Blakely Bey stated that the Holy Prophet said "*Many of you who think you are running away from the Prophet don't know that the further you run away from me, the closer you are coming to me, and when you wind up running you will be right in my arms.*"

248. See page 101.

249. Bro. J. Blakely Bey stated that the Holy Prophet said "*Celebrate my birthday January the 8th, invite your Asiatic friends to come out and enjoy it with you. Yes, bring out your baskets of food to the Temple and banquet them.*"

250. Bro. J. Blakely Bey stated that the Holy Prophet said "*These Verbal Laws are Everlasting and Eternal just as much as my Written Laws.*"

251. See page 101.

252. The Holy Prophet once stated that "*The grand body shall make the laws and the supreme council shall interpret the laws and be the sole judges of what constitute a violation of the laws that are made.*"

253. Bro. Edward Mealy El stated that the Holy Prophet said "*I have my number, and my work of redeeming you people is finished, and I must now go, or I can't return; and if I don't return, I can't deliver you, and if I don't deliver you, then my coming is in vain.*"

254. See page 102.

255. Bro. Edward Mealy El stated that the Holy prophet told him "*You do what I tell you, never mind what they say, I have given you Law, Koran, and Constitution, and I expect you to enforce my Law and do I say, never mind what 'they' say or do. 'They' can do nothing but die.*"

256. Bro. Edward Mealy El stated that The Holy Prophet told him "*Children, there won't be but a few saved; because you are not going to do what I tell you. You way you want, and your way you are going to have. But your way leads downward Children;*

so you better do like I tell you. If you do like I tell you, there is a chance for you, if not; there is nothing for you, but death."

257. The Holy Prophet said *"They will take this movement down so low; it will disappear from the face of the earth."*

258. *See page 102.*

259. The Prophet was quoted as saying *"Asiatic Preachers and Masons will be the last to come home. They will fight me tooth and claw but cannot win."*

Notes

Other Titles Available from Califa Media®

77 Amazing Facts About the Moors

Holistic Philosophy 101

Isonomi: The Great Masonic Secret: Master Keys

Moorish Children's Guide to History and Culture

Moorish Jewels: Emerald Ed

Moors in America

Moslem Girls' Training Guide a.k.a. The Sisters' Auxiliary Handbook

Nationality, the Order of the Day

Noble Drew Ali Plenipotentiaries

Official Proclamation of Real Moorish American Nationality

Well, Come to Klanada

Califa Uhuru Series

Vol. 1: Holy Koran of the Moorish Holy Temple of Science, Circle 7

Vol. 2: "I'm Going to Repeat Myself.": A Collection of Artifacts Authored by Noble Prophet Drew Ali and the M.S.T. of A.

Vol. 3: Mysteries of the Silent Brotherhood of the East a.k.a. The Red Book, a.k.a. Sincerity

Vol. 4: Califa Uhuru; A Collection of Literature from the Moorish Science Temple of America

www.ingramcontent.com/pod-product-compliance
Lightning Source LLC
Chambersburg PA
CBHW030154100526
44592CB00009B/279